Celebrating the
Art of Architecture

25 Years of Pritzker Prize
Winning Architects

Celebrating the
Art of Architecture

25 Years of Pritzker Prize Winning Architects

Jaye Abbate

Michael C. Thomsett

MARKETPLACE BOOKS
Columbia, MD

This book, along with many other books, is available at discounts that make it realistic to provide them as gifts to your customers, clients, and staff. For more information on these long lasting, cost effective premiums, please call John Boyer at (800) 272-2855 or you may email him at John@architecturebookdeals.com

ISBN 1-59280-148-X

Printed in the United States of America.

1 2 3 4 5 6 7 8 9 0

Contents

Introduction   Architecture — The Mother of All Arts 7

Chapter 1   The "Dean of Architects" 13
Philip C. Johnson, 1979 Laureate

Chapter 2   A Sense of Restful Sensuality 23
Luis Barragán, 1980 Laureate

Chapter 3   The Color of White 33
Richard Meier, 1984 Laureate

Chapter 4   The "Other" Frank 43
Frank Gehry, 1989 Laureate

Chapter 5   Deceptive Simplicity 53
Álvaro Siza, 1992 Laureate

Chapter 6   Places of Serene Possibility 61
Tadao Ando, 1995 Laureate

Chapter 7   A Magician — Rooted in the Believable 69
Renzo Piano, 1998 Laureate

Chapter 8   Romancing the Skyscraper 79
Sir Norman Foster, 1999 Laureate

Chapter 9   A Complete Original 89
Rem Koolhaas, 2000 Laureate

Chapter 10   A Mandate of Unpredictability 99
Zaha Hadid, 2004 Laureate

Conclusion   Architecture — A Mythical Fantastic 107

Appendix   Pritzker Architecture Prize Winners: 1979-2004 109

Credits   Notes & Photo Credits 113

Other   Recommended Reading 121

"The mother art is architecture. Without an architecture of our own, we have no soul of our own civilization."

— Frank Lloyd Wright

Architecture —
The Mother of All Arts

In 1979, the architecture world finally got its due. The Pritzker Architecture Prize, which has become to architecture what the Nobel Prize is to literature, was established in 1979 by The Hyatt Foundation. Its mission is to honor annually a living architect whose body of work has produced significant contributions to humanity and the built environment, through "the art of architecture." It is undeniably the most prestigious award in the architecture profession, and the stature it has placed on the value of architecture in our society has enlightened the masses, and provided much deserved recognition to one of the most important of art forms.

Architecture is, in fact, the art form that affects our lives *most*. Yet, it also tends to be the most overlooked art form. Why? Because we take it for granted. Everyday we enter, exit, and experience the buildings in which we live, work, shop, and worship . . . but we do so without ever being truly conscious of how they affect us. In essence, we often look at them without *seeing* them.

But that situation will, hopefully, be changing. The Pritzker Architecture Prize has made a major contribution to raising the awareness of the contribution architecture makes to the quality of our daily lives, to our society, and to motivating new architects to aspire to even greater accomplishments.

It is hard to believe that until 1979 there was no international award to honor noteworthy achievements in architecture. The professional associations recognized their peers. The Nobel acknowledged other art forms. However, no distinction was made for architecture, even though it is, as Frank Lloyd Wright so famously called it, "the mother of all arts." 1979 The Pritzker family, through their Hyatt Foundation, changed that injustice and started a grand tradition of celebrating annually "the art of architecture."

The prize takes its name from the Pritzker family who

founded the Hyatt Hotel chain and whose international business interests are headquartered in Chicago. They have long been known for their philanthropic work and generous support of educational, religious, medical, social and cultural activities. In 1979, Jay A. Pritzker, with his wife Cindy, established the prize in response to a personal experience and to fill a void in the art world. After the death of his father in 1999, Thomas J. Pritzker became president of the Hyatt Foundation and continues the mission begun by his parents.

In 1967, Thomas Pritzker relates, his company "acquired an unfinished building which was to become the Hyatt Regency Atlanta. Its soaring atrium was wildly successful and became the signature piece of our hotels around the world. It was immediately apparent that this design had a pronounced affect on the mood of guests and [the] attitude of our employees."[1] And so, they became far more attuned to the power architecture has to transform moods, productivity and our daily lives in general.

"As native Chicagoans," he further explains, "it's not surprising that our family was keenly aware of architecture, living in the birthplace of the skyscraper, a city filled with buildings designed by architectural legends such as Louis Sullivan, Frank Lloyd Wright, Mies van der Rohe, and many others. While the architecture of Chicago made us cognizant of the art of architecture," he continues, "our work with designing and building hotels made us aware of the impact architecture could have on human behavior."

The Hyatt Foundation used the Nobel Prize procedures as the model for their award, granting each laureate a $100,00 cash prize, a formal citation and, since

1987, a bronze medallion. Before that year, a limited edition Henry Moore sculpture was presented to each recipient.

Nominations are accepted from all nations, writers, academicians, fellow architects, architectural societies, and government bodies, virtually anyone who might have an interest in advancing great architecture. The prize is awarded irrespective of nationality, race, creed, or ideology — and it's been bestowed on architects of wide international acclaim as well as modest practitioners, architects from small countries, and those with a limited body of work known outside their region. Quality, and a major contribution to the art of architecture, are the only essential requirements. The nominating procedure is continuous from year to year, closing in January, and the final selection is made by an international jury that conducts all deliberations and voting in secret.

The presentation award ceremonies are held in a different location around the world each year — in an effort to honor significant buildings of the past, as well as those of living architects — including venues designed by many former Pritzker Prize winners. The locales have become almost an architectural tour of the world's great buildings.

The Pritzker Architecture Prize recipients themselves comprise a veritable Who's Who of modern architecture and include the best designers of their generation. Beginning with Philip Johnson, the first honoree, their work embodies in every

"While the architecture of Chicago made us cognizant of the art of architecture, our work with designing and building hotels made us aware of the impact architecture could have on human behavior."

— Thomas Pritzker

way the true essence of the award. They have life-long dedication to upholding the highest standards of their industry, to making our world a more beautiful and habitable place, ensuring there is humanity in all of their work and to instilling the creative spirit in everything they do.

While the award presentations have become glamorous over the years, even star-making affairs, they have provided a wonderful showcase for many lesser-known talents around the world and have made a true celebration of the art of architecture.

In the pages that follow, you will be introduced to a

small group of Pritzker Prize Laureates, as a way of illustrating the several key qualities possessed by the entire group. These ten were selected because they show the variety of the recipients, the difference in their personal styles and aesthetics, the various developments within the profession that have occurred over the years and, ultimately, how the collective contributions of all winners have affected our lives.

This book is by no means a comprehensive treatment of their work, or of architecture itself. Nor does it list all the major projects of the architects profiled, since so many detailed accounts are readily available. In fact, this book does not even feature every award winner to date. While each and every one deserves to be singled out, only a handful were selected as a way of representing the scope and diversity of all Pritzker Prize winners over the years.

We open with Philip Johnson, the generation-spanning "dean of architects," who was the first Pritzker Prize Laureate. Johnson is followed by Luis Barragán who, along with Álvaro Siza, was selected to illustrate how the jury recognizes the achievements of architects who are highly praised in their own regions, but whose body of work is less known on an international scale. They also reinforce the impact regional architects have on future generations across the globe, by virtue of their often groundbreaking work.

Richard Meier and Tadao Ando represent the movement to mix modern, minimalist architecture with nature to create places of serene beauty. In contrast, Renzo Piano, who pioneered the High-Tech look, and Sir Norman Foster, who has taken it to the next level with his ecologically-conscious, ever-taller buildings, are both featured due to the enormous impact they've had on modern building design, thanks to advances in technology.

Rem Koolhaas, who was the Pritzker choice to usher in the new millennium, was chosen because he represents a new breed of multi-tasking architects, since he is known as much for his books, writings and theories as for his built work. And his one-time colleague, Zaha Hadid, the 2004 recipient is, to state the obvious, the first female to receive the award. More importantly, though she is a unique, cutting-edge practitioner who shows how perseverance and belief in one's own vision can become reality.

Finally, Frank Gehry, who seems destined to become as admired and beloved as "the other Frank"— Frank Lloyd Wright—is among the ten profiled because he embodies all of the qualities the Pritzker Prize cherishes. He is an artist, a sculptor, and a humble humanitarian. His buildings soar, he inspires his colleagues—and he enriches our collective experience.

As "the other Frank"—Frank Lloyd Wright—has said, "Without an architecture of our own, we have no soul of our own civilization." All Pritzker honorees, not just those featured in this volume, give soul to our generation.

Thomas Pritzker and his family recognized that architecture—the mother of all arts—has the power to affect human behavior, to move and transform people, and when done well, make people both look *and* see. Perhaps one of the founding Pritzker Prize jurors expressed it best. Kenneth Clark, who gained worldwide fame for his television series and book, *Civilisation*, explained:

> **A great historical episode can exist in our imagination almost entirely in the form of architecture. Very few of us have read the texts of early Egyptian literature. Yet we feel we know those infinitely remote people almost as well as our immediate ancestors, chiefly because of their sculpture and architecture.[2]**

That is the power of architecture. And the recipients of the coveted prize featured in this work—as well as each and every one we've been forced to overlook—have this kind of power, and live up to the high ideals set forth in 1979. They all celebrate the art of architecture. And in the chapters that follow, so can we all. ◼

"The practice of architecture is the most delightful of pursuits. Also, next to agriculture, it is the most necessary to man. One must eat, one must have shelter ... Even more than painting and sculpture, it is *the* primary art of our, or any other, culture."

— Philip C. Johnson

CHAPTER 1

The "Dean of Architects"

Philip C. Johnson (1906-   )
1979 Laureate

The Pritzker Prize jury could not have found a more fitting recipient to become the very first laureate in 1979. At seventy-three, Johnson's resume truly embodied the spirit of the prize itself — both through his profound impact on the direction and intellectual dialogue about architecture, as well as his actual contributions to the built environment.

His rich body of work had spanned nearly five decades by 1979, and his reputation was that of a colorful living legend. He was opinionated, provocative and always controversial. But even his detractors were quick to acknowledge his enormous contributions to the field throughout most of the twentieth century, and into the twenty-first. Few would have guessed that a good twenty-five years later he would still be a dynamic force on the architecture scene.

Johnson's personal evolution over the past seventy years has advanced on a surprisingly parallel track with that of the art and architecture world during

"Glass walls make people feel comfortable because they are connected with their environment and their surroundings." — Philip C. Johnson

the same period. In fact, he's often acted as a catalyst for new schools of thought, or new trends in building. His passion has been unyielding and undiminished even as he approaches the one hundred year mark.

In his acceptance speech at the Pritzker Prize award ceremony, Johnson spoke of the thrill he gets from creating a building. He noted that "whole civilizations are remembered by their buildings; indeed some *only* by their buildings." The inauguration of the prize, Johnson hoped, would set off a building "Renaissance" that would "shape our surroundings in a way this generation will be remembered, as others have been, as great builders."

The extensive list of Johnson's projects, his life-long devotion to art and architecture, and the indelible mark he's left on both, will ensure that this and every generation to follow will remember him as one of the "great builders" he spoke of —and one of the architecture world's great innovators.

Born in Cleveland, Ohio in 1906, Johnson did not design his first building until age thirty-six — when many architects are already well into their profession. Instead, his pathway to prominence began on a much different track.

Johnson launched his career as an architecture author, critic, and historian in the 1930s. After traveling extensively throughout Europe in his twenties, he became one of the first to study and champion the new school of modern European architecture, referred to as the International Style. His passion for this new approach culminated in a book and exhibition on International Style at the Museum of Modern Art in New York, where he was the founding director of the architecture department. A strong advocate of the European modernists from the Bauhaus School, Johnson formed strong alliances with many Bauhaus key figures including Walter Gropius, Le Corbusier and, most notably, Mies van der Rohe, with whom he later collaborated on several projects.

Not satisfied with being just the primary publicist of the modernist movement in America, Johnson then became one of its first American practitioners. In the early 1940s, he turned his efforts away from merely writing about architecture, to becoming a practicing architect in his own right. He received his professional degree in architecture from Harvard in 1943, and in 1949 designed the now famous "Glass House" in New Canaan, Connecticut for his master's degree thesis. This sumptuously transparent steel-and-glass-walled house reveals the enormous influence of Mies van der Rohe on Johnson's early work. It has since become one of the most significant and most photographed designs of the last century, and a true showcase of classic modern architecture. It has also served as Johnson's permanent residence.

BELOW:
The Glass House,
New Canaan,
Connecticut, 1949.

"The inescapable drama of the Seagram Building in a city already dramatic with crowded skyscrapers lies in its unbroken height of bronze and dark glass juxtaposed to a granite-paved plaza below."

—A. James Speyer

Throughout the 1950s Johnson continued to support and collaborate with Mies. He paid for Mies' first visit to the U.S. and commissioned Mies to design his New York apartment. He eventually teamed up with Mies on what has been described as this continent's finest high-rise structure, the Seagram Building in New York City (1958). This 38-story project's "perfectly proportioned, utterly simple slab of dark bronze and amber-tinted glass-curtain walls set a style, as did the opulently named granite plaza behind which it is set."[1] In addition, it set the design tone for all the post-war skyscrapers that were soon to follow.

With an extensive list of skyscrapers to his name Johnson's pared-down Penzoil Place in Houston, Texas broke entirely new ground as well, and redefined the role archi-

RIGHT: Penzoil Place, Houston, Texas, 1976.

16

"We eschew old-fashioned words like "God, soul, aesthetics, glory, monumentality, beauty. We like practical words like cost-effective, businesslike, profitable." — Philip C. Johnson

tecture would play in the business world. This sleek steel-and-glass tower with its clean lines and "trapezoids with sliced-off tops" was able to prove that "quality architecture could bring a large economic return for developers."[2] This concept ushered in a whole new way of looking at the "business of architecture" — and architecture as business — that came to dominate the modern way of building to this very day. As Johnson was later to claim, "We eschew old-fashioned words like God, soul, aesthetics, glory, monumentality, beauty. We like practical words like cost-effective, businesslike, profitable."[3]

Johnson, however, was never one to remain static. He has always enjoyed being able to stir things up, try new things and, in his own words "go against the grain." By the 1960s, Johnson started turning away from the purist International Style he had once so devoutly followed. He began imbuing his modern buildings with historical references, such as the Ottoman Empire-inspired domed circles found on the Museum for Pre-Columbian Art in Washington, D.C. (1963). By the 1970s, Johnson's break with the glass box, functionalism, rationalism and the universal notions of modernism was complete. He embraced a new school of architecture that was at once familiar, historical and vernacular. He would take a modern skyscraper and then apply columns, arches, and other classical styles of the past that performed no functional purpose. This new approach became known as Postmodernism.

Johnson's split with his modernist roots and his gravitation towards Postmodernism is manifested most prominently in his 1979 AT&T headquarters in New York (now called the Sony Building). AT&T — with its classical façade, symmetry of elements, arched entryway, large columns in the lobby, and crowned with its "Chippendale" top — was postmodernism as its most eccentric and controversial. While eschewed by legions of "less is more" modernists as mere decoration or ornamentation, Postmodernism was legitimized by Johnson, prompting Robert Venturi's "less is a bore" rebuttal.

"What's fun in life is to change," Johnson has been known to have said, and Johnson continued to evolve. With his partner, John Burgee, he courted powerful developers as clients and attracted numerous high-profile projects from Minneapolis' IDS Center (1973), to the elegant and majestic Crystal Cathedral in Garden Grove, California (1980). This massive building, which serves as the headquarters for Robert Schuller's televangelism ministry, was original-

Postmodernism

Johnson would take a modern skyscraper and then apply columns, arches, and other classical styles of the past that performed no functional purpose. This new approach became known as Postmodernism.

LEFT:
Crystal Cathedral
Garden Grove, California,
1980.

OPPOSITE PAGE:
AT&T Headquarters,
New York, 1979.

ly intended to reside in a park-like setting, but today it overlooks a paved parking lot. In true California style, sections of the exterior walls open up so that people can view services without leaving the comfort of their own cars. "I love to do churches," Johnson has said, "because there is a spatial feeling of God that you have going for you that's a little more interesting than the layers of office cubicles."[4]

In 1978, Philip Johnson received the Gold Medal of the American Institute of Architects—the highest honor of his profession at the time. The following year he won the first Pritzker Architecture Prize for lifetime achievement. But his body of significant work was by no means winding down. During his partnership with John Burgee from 1967 through 1987, their twenty-year output was phenomenal, producing a staggering number of significant—primarily high

> **"Once I discovered** architecture as a need of my nature, that enthusiasm knew no bounds and it's been the same ever since . . . Art is the only thing I've been alive for."

rise — buildings around the world, and testing the waters in a wide range of architecture genres.

Johnson then went on to devote much of his time to his own projects, and the commissions kept coming. Though he's known as one of the most influential architects of the twentieth century, he's never considered himself on par with past masters such as Frank Lloyd Wright, Le Corbusier or his former collaborator Mies van der Rohe. "I'm not a form giver," he has said, "but we're not in an age of form-giving. My contribution has been working with younger architects."[5]

And, to a large extent, this is true. Just as he introduced a generation of Americans in the 1930's to the modern day European masters of the International School such as Mies van der Rohe, he was equally influential in the 1970's for mentoring into prominence a new generation of architects — Peter Eisenman, John Hejduk, Michael Graves, Charles Gwathmey, and Richard Meier. Collectively, the five constituted a "New York school" of architecture and, under Johnson's tutelage, they began to receive some of the most significant commissions of their day. A generation later, all five are now among the most influential architects working today.

The common denominator they shared with Johnson, though, is their absolute passion for the art of architecture. Despite their personal theories, or varied individual visions, all five simply shared a keen fervor for architecture and they would meet regularly to discuss, theorize and debate it.

In the 1990s, Johnson again embraced a new movement in architecture, ushered in by the exciting deconstructionist work of architects like Frank Gehry, Rem Koolhaas and Zaha Hadid. And in the new century, Johnson has continued to revel in change, preferring to design in a variety of modes rather than aligning himself solely with one school or another. From an historical "folly" in Vermont to a huge urban redevelopment project in Liverpool, England, Johnson "keeps it fun" by keeping it fresh. He's also, in a way, come nearly full circle. As a testament to his enduring legacy, Philip Johnson and his colleague Alan Ritchie have recently been commissioned to build an "Urban Glass House" in New York City. This eleven-story transparent residential building in Lower Manhattan will draw heavily on the design elements of Johnson's signature building, the original "glass house" which remains his Connecticut residence. In addition, "The streetscape will also reflect the historic designs of Philip Johnson such as those for the Gardens at the Museum of Modern Art."[6]

Johnson has been referred to over the years as "architecture's great chameleon" for quickly embracing every passing fad or new architectural style. He's even shamelessly referred to himself as a "whore." But he's also been heralded by many as the one who's successfully, over the years, anticipated "the next great thing."

And no matter how people evaluate his talents as an architect, no one can dispute Johnson's commitment to the "quality of the built environment and to beauty." He is an ardent art collector and strong advocate of historic preservation. But his legacy will surely be the two architectural movements that he had a profound impact on encouraging, and which have altered the urban landscape over the past sixty years: The International Style and the reintroduction of historic styles into contemporary architectural design.

American architect, museum curator, historian, art collector — and architecture's elder statesman — Philip Johnson is still going strong at nearly one hundred years of age. Through his designs, writings, and teachings he has played a seminal role in defining the shape and form of architecture in the twentieth century, and his life's work has more than adequately fulfilled the Pritzker Prize's mission to enrich humanity and the built environment through the art of architecture. With almost prophetic foresight, the first Pritzker was bestowed on an architect whose influence would span nearly a century. And how fortuitous that as a boy Johnson dreamed of writing the history of architecture — and then went on to play such a significant role in creating that history himself. ■

"Any work of architecture which does not express serenity is a mistake."

— Luis Barragán

CHAPTER 2

A Sense of Restful Sensuality

Luis Barragán (1902-1988)
1980 Laureate

If the Pritzker Prize was meant to celebrate the "art" of architecture — with an emphasis on "art" — then the 1980 honoree, Mexican architect Luis Barragán, was an ideal choice. It is difficult to find a single reference to Barragán's work that does not describe it as "poetic," "colorful," "spiritual" or "serene" — terms more typically associated with artistic endeavors such as poetry or painting, rather than architecture.

The 1980 Pritzker jury members used this language when they praised Luis Barragán for his "sublime act of poetic imagination. He has created gardens, plazas and fountains of haunting beauty — metaphysical landscapes for meditation and companionship."

In stark contrast to the Pritzker's prior recipient, the gregarious, ever-changing Philip Johnson who was so visible on the international architecture scene — Barragán was a gentle, unassuming figure in the architecture world who worked primarily in his native Mexico. And while his early projects were designed in the International Style first popularized by Johnson, Barragán soon found working within the confines of that school too restrictive. He went on, as most true masters do, to develop a style all his own.

Rather than imposing a foreign façade on his country, Barragán sought to merge elements of his native land with methods and styles from the outside. What resulted is one of the most important, original and admired bodies of architecture of the twentieth century, which is appreciated and acclaimed to this day.

While in his twenties, Luis Barragán left Mexico and traveled extensively throughout Europe and North Africa. There he was exposed to Mediterranean and Moorish architecture, which is reflected in much of his early work. He was also influenced by his exposure to Le Corbusier and the International Style which further manifested itself in his first projects. But as time went on, he became critical of the stark modern International School. "I believe that much of what we have been doing over the last fifteen or twenty years is essentially academic, with no real exploration of new forms," he said. "Some 'homes' are in fact simply glass boxes, or rather cubes . . . Perhaps that is why we so often want to 'go out,' to get away from our houses. We have lost our sense of intimate life . . ."[1]

The most profound and lasting impact on Barragán during this early period was the writings of French landscape architect Ferdinand Bac who espoused the theory that the garden was a sacred space, "an enchanted place for meditation that should 'bewitch' the onlooker."[2] Barragán found an immediate bond with Bac's emphasis on the interplay of the design process with the natural environment. The art of landscaping soon began to guide his personal philosophy and approach to architecture. Through Bac's teachings, Barragán gained a better understanding of how the elements of building — the beams, roof-tiles, arches and room connections — interact with the natural environment — the rocks, stones, water and natural light. Barragán, like Bac, felt that "the garden should present a peaceful place of repose — and the building is a mere tool in achieving this serene connection." Unlike his contemporaries, his emphasis on "the garden as a magical environment" literally transformed his structures from that time on. By the mid-1940s Barragán's architecture projects increasingly focused on land-

"The garden is the myth of the Beginning, and the chapel that of the End. For Barragán, architecture is the form man gives to his life between both extremes."

— Citation from the Pritzker Jury

scape architecture as well—combining the two in a way not seen before and "designing streets, pools, pathways and fountains in a manner that deferred to natural rock formations"[3] — and the existing environment.

He also, at this time, "discovered his country." He sought to form his own unique sense of Mexican regionalism, drawing on its vernacular roots, but going one step further by imbuing it with his romantic notion of landscape architecture. Barragán mined a multitude of influences and sources to accomplish this — reaching back to the serenity and beauty of his early Mexican childhood, his love for native artwork, the minimal aesthetic of the modernists and, most important-ly, the connection between the interior and the exterior.

As his close friend and long-time collaborator Ignacio Diaz Morales notes, "He closed his ears so as not to hear any song other than that of his own intuition. He paid no attention to outside suggestions or stimuli and avoided the posture of any school. Against wind and tide, he was the creator of architecture, of his own architecture."[4]

By 1945, the realization of this personal vision started to take shape when he purchased a large track of desert land which was covered in lava remains from an ancient volcanic eruption. Working as both architect and developer, he shaped this raw, otherworldly landscape into one of his signature projects. He viewed this design challenge, called El Pedregal, largely as a landscape exercise that incorporated into the environment houses, parks and fountains, rather than as a building project that viewed the landscape as accessory. El Pedregal demonstrated his unique ability to form a symbiotic relationship between nature and architecture and create spaces of serene and powerful beauty. It is a philosophy that architects to this day study and try to emulate.

While many architects of the time were exploring European trends of the International Style, mimicking modern American movements or working within strictly vernacular vocabularies, Barragán searched solely for "the essence of architecture as the work of art which consists of expressive space, delineated by constructive elements which compel the perfect human act."[5]

This idea carried over to all his future works including, his renowned residential project, Luis Barragán House (*Casa de Luis Barragán*) in Tacubaya, Mexico. It appears, at first, quiet and unpretentious. However, beyond its stark facade, the Barragán house is a showplace for his use of color, form, texture, light and

"Luis Barragán, you will always be remembered for the poetry and beauty you brought to architecture . . . emotion will always arise when beholding the Xitle and its Pedregal. The earth fashioned a wild garden and you made it habitable. Your works extol the reality we live in."

—Armando Salas Portugal

shadow.[6] — all themes that can be found in the majority of his designs that followed. Tranquil spaces created through cubic areas with textured walls, variations on platforms, patio areas and terraces, and secret garden areas are all found in this work. Another intriguing design element is the ambiguous plane — Barragán's ability to control how the viewer's eye sees an area. The layers of space are designed with reflecting pools and the use of natural light, but that light often comes from hidden sources rather than from direct sunlight. The seclusion of this site, created with minimal openings and dense walls, defines a theme that Barragán called emotional architecture.

That emotional effect is not limited to the garden areas, however. The inside of *Casa Luis Barragán* has been called "a space of spiritual absorption." One article described it as "a place to be and enjoy life in a different manner, far away from the world . . . [Barragán's] work is divorced from conventional lines and develops a language in which he balances a delicate harmonious relationship between his elements."[7]

Barragán further extended this philosophy to the numerous stables and water troughs he designed, employing rich colors and textures that were in harmony with nature and created spaces that project a unique sense of serenity. A fellow architect described her first impression of Barragán's style on a visit to Mexico as follows: "It was exquisite. It captured the time and the place, the texture and contents of its surroundings. It was, in a word, poetry."[8]

A sense of spirituality is also inescapable in Barragán's houses. They have been depicted as places "monastic in spirit" which "provided a refuge from contemporary life. The closely integrated interior and exterior spaces were surrounded by walls designed to create a private and serene environment. Window sizes were limited except when facing a private courtyard, with its pool and fountain." [9] Barragán himself best explained the artis-

"Another great lesson

tic and creative force that guides him when he noted that, "Architecture, besides being spatial, is also musical. That music is played with water. The importance of walls is that they isolate one from the street's exterior space. The street is aggressive, even hostile. Walls create silence. From that silence you can play with water as music. Afterwards, that music surrounds us."[10]

A Barragán work can often be identified by the inventive use of abstract planes, sliding water surfaces, and his ability to create the illusion of space by using brilliant combinations of color and natural light. And though bright, contrasting colors in the wrong hands can stimulate, Barragán's work is tranquil and relaxing, while at the same time poetic. His ability to create these amazing spaces through simple techniques can also be attributed to his unique ability to "see." He referred to the "art of seeing" in Pritzker Prize acceptance speech, claiming that "it is essential to an architect to know how to see: I mean to see in such a way that the vision is not overpowered by rational analysis." Instead, Barragán's work found its profound beauty in architectural simplicity, in nature and in art rather than in the more practical considerations.

Because so little of his remarkable landscaping work has survived, Barragán is most widely known for his houses. And though he worked primarily in Mexico and was never as prolific as many of his counterparts, his work has had an enormous impact on architects around the globe, including many of the most famous who continue to study it and marvel over what he was able to achieve by his simple, humble manner and technique. As the eminent archi-

of Luis Barragán is that great architecture is derived from the interrelation of three systems: creation . . . the city . . . and the building, which together formulate a super ecosystem, an accord between nature, the human community and the individual."

— Ignacio Diaz Morales

29

tect and designer Massimo Vignelli has stated: "The incredibly beautiful abstract representation of Barragán's walls, the terrace of his own house, the fountains and walls of Los Clubes, or the courtyards of El Pedregal and San Critstobal have indeed become powerful icons which have enriched our perception, fueled our inspiration and transformed our work."[11]

In stark contrast to Philip Johnson, his Pritzker Prize predecessor, Luis Barragán shunned technical and functional aspects of modern architecture, preferring to emphasize poetic and spiritual expression. Though his architecture is sometimes seen as "minimal," Barragán explained that it is serenity as much as spirituality that influenced him: "I believe that architects should design gardens to be used, as much as the houses they build, to develop a sense of beauty and the taste and inclination toward the fine arts and spiritual values. . . . Any work of architecture which does not express serenity is a mistake."[12]

"Barragán leaves his trace in what he builds . . . We who know Barragán can affirm, without any doubt, that this man is greater than his architecture."

—Ricardo Legorreta

"The greatest lesson that Luis Barragán gave us is that whoever has a mind for creation can cultivate it with humility."

—Ignacio Diaz Morales

And much as his Pritzker predecessor Philip Johnson was shedding a realistic eye on the penetration of the business culture into the world of architecture, Barragán never wavered from his personal view of architecture as art. In his acceptance speech, Barragán called it "alarming that publications devoted to architecture seemed to have banished the words Beauty, Inspiration, Magic, Spellbound, Enchantment as well as the concepts of Serenity, Silence, Intimacy and Amazement." While noting that all of these "have found a loving home in my soul," he humbly apologized for not having done these concepts complete justice, but assured the audience that "they have never ceased to be my guiding lights."

And indeed, in his gentle and powerful way he has continued to be a guiding light to the many fine architects who continue to study and marvel at his modest, dignified and utterly moving creations. ■

"We are all affected by Le Corbusier, Frank Lloyd Wright, Alvar Aalto, and Mies van der Rohe. But no less than Bramante, Borromini and Bernini. Architecture is a tradition, a long continuum. Whether we break with tradition or enhance it, we are still connected to that past. We evolve."

— Richard Meier

CHAPTER 3

The Color of White

Richard Meier (1934-   )
1984 Laureate

White. If there's a single word that is most associated with the 1984 Pritzker Laureate Richard Meier, many would say it is "white." White is his favorite color. It's a consistent theme in all of his work. It's a continuing source of inspiration for him. And while Luis Barragán showed the world how the richness of color can be used to create powerful, serene spaces, pure white is the palette from which Richard Meier's marvelous creations have emerged.

Meier first came to prominence on a national scale as a member of the Neo-Corbusian "New York Five." His work, along with that of fellow New York architects Peter Eisenman, Charles Gwathmey, John Hejduk and Michael Graves, was exhibited at New York's Museum of Modern Art in 1969. A book entitled *Five Architects*, published in 1972, outlined their theoretical and ideological discourse. The "five" traced their modernist concepts on "autonomous" architecture back to the foundations of Le Corbusier. Emulating the International Style with simple

Architecture as art.

Vienna based Hans Hollein, 1985 Pritzker Laureate, shares with Meier a reverence and respect for nature, harmonizing his designs within their natural surroundings. But, as the Pritzker jury noted, "he mingles bold shapes and colors with an exquisite refinement of detail and never fears to bring together the richest of ancient marbles and the latest in plastics," thus drawing "upon the traditions of the New World as readily as upon those of the Old." An architect who is also an artist, Hollein's structures are as untamed and colorful as Meier's are classic and subdued. They are, noted the Pritzker jury, "Gigantic in scale and scope," and in keeping with the mission of the prize, they "decried functionalism, the ruling aesthetic of the day, and claimed the right . . . to consider architecture as an art."[1]

volumes, formal clarity, absence of ornament and, most notably, flat white surfaces, they were frequently referred to as "the whites." Many of "the five" eventually experimented in other genres and moved on to favor different paradigms. Richard Meier, however, has remained faithful to his purist roots, continuing unabated to create works that are at once stunning, exciting and restful.

However, while Meier has remained true to classification as one of the "white" architects, reducing his work to a mere word or description does it a tremendous disservice. Though Meier has continued to design in a very concise architectural vocabulary, he has also managed to produce endless variations on this singular theme and continues to surprise and delight.

At the age of 49, Richard Meier was the youngest Pritzker Prize laureate when he received his award in 1984 — and his most prestigious commissions were *yet* to come. But even at this early stage in his career, Meier had proven himself to be one of the most preeminent architects of the twentieth century, and a most worthy recipient.

After completing his education at Cornell University and working with a series of prominent architects, including Marcel Breuer and Skidmore, Ownings and Merrill, Meier established his own practice in 1963 with a commission from his parents to design a residence for them in Essex Fells, New Jersey.

The Smith House (1967), in Darien, Connecticut soon followed, and ultimately put Meier on the map for paying "homage to the villas of Le Corbusier while at the same time carefully integrating his buildings into their natural environments." Though a routinely accepted practice today, the harmony of design and natural elements was considered somewhat groundbreaking when introduced by Meier in the sixties. As he later recalled, "It's been over seventeen years, and what was innovative and captured a great many people's imagination and admiration then, is already part of our language, and somewhat taken for granted today."[2] Several attributes of the Smith House, including the "clarity of the building, the openness, the direct articulation of private and public spaces, how it relates to the land and the water," dominate the many private residences he designed during this period.

"There is a formal layering, giving a sense of progression, as one moves across the site from the entrance road down to the shore, and the 'line of progression' determines the major site axis. Perpendicular to this axis, the intersecting planes in the house respond to the rhythms of the slope, trees, rock outcroppings, and the shoreline."

— Richard Meier.
Richard Meier, Architect. New York: Oxford University Press, 1976. p23

35

Meier's next major breakthrough came when working on the conversion of the old Bell Telephone Laboratories in Manhattan's Greenwich Village to apartment units. It was widely praised in the architectural community as a true innovation. As Meier later noted, 'This, too, is an example of how quickly we assimilate . . . the phrase 'adaptive re-use' wasn't even in the language then. We were really pioneering a new area."[3]

The Atheneum Visitor's Center in New Harmony, Indiana, completed in 1979, broke new ground again and prompted architecture critic Ada Louise Huxtable to declare that it advanced "conventional modernist practice provocatively beyond established limits." Meier managed to incorporate many of his signature themes into this project, which is situated on the banks of the Wabash River. Its glass walls create a feeling of openness and keep key spaces, such as the theater, visible. Large windows frame views of the town and connect the interior spaces to the lush outdoor landscape. Daring planes, ramps, glass walls, columns and curving lines are all assembled in a complex arrangement enveloped by a striking white porcelain box of grids. Visitors arriving by foot or river are greeted, as in his earlier work, by an amazing three-dimensional structure that relates seamlessly with its surroundings. Clad in white, it continued Meier's exploration of this means of expression which he went on to achieve on an even grander scale with the High Museum of Art project in Atlanta, Georgia.

The High, completed in 1983, won Meier international acclaim and he thereafter became a significant force as an architect of museums and other public works. The dramatic orthogonal sweep of white porcelain-enameled panels is at once a standard Meier feature and a fresh new interpretation. Set strategically off the street to delay the approach and enhance the visitor's appreciation of the structure, it blends into and accents the building's natural surrounding. By creating the perfect balance of space and light, Meier's design enables the museum management to adjust the degree of light as specific exhibit requirements dictate, and enriches the space for all who enter. Meier described the visual intention of his design was "to foster a contemplative appreciation of the museum's collection through its own spatial experience."[4]

The High was followed by anther significant museum project, the Museum of Decorative Arts (Museum fur Kunsthandwerk) in Frankfurt, Germany (1981-1984), which was deliberately and intentionally harmonious with nature and represented the intersections of geometrics with the neighborhood setting.

ABOVE:
The High Museum of Art,
Atlanta, Georgia, 1983.

"The museum is emphatically a public and an urban institution, a rejection of modernist isolation of the building as a free-standing object distanced from its surrounds. The scheme here is meant to connect: to respond to, enlarge, and reinforce the public context and the urban fabric."[5]

Meier's extensive body of work up to this point in his career, which earned him architecture's highest honor in 1984, prompted the Pritzker committee to cite him for his "Single-minded pursuit of the essence of modern architecture," commenting that he had "broadened its range of forms to make it responsive to the expectations of our time. In his search for clarity and his experiments balancing light and space, he has created structures which are personal, vigorous, and original."[6]

The years since his award have become his busiest and most prolific, and throughout, Meier has successfully adapted his characteristic design aesthetic to a remarkable body of works around the globe. From The Hague, to projects in Barcelona, Paris, and Rome his work has remained true to his neo-modern beliefs in purist design, and utterly original at the same time. Running through all his projects is his sense of aesthetic pureness manifested by the perpetual use of his favorite color, white.

Far from making his work bland or boring by the continual use of just one color, Meier has found inventive ways to add contrast and resolution by layering, using sculptured grids, and creating molded, complex spaces infused with abundant natural light. This can best be seen in what many consider his crowning achievement, The Getty Center in Brentwood, California (1997).

At a cost of over one billion dollars, the Getty Center is a sprawling complex of buildings on a hilltop campus that includes a museum, library, research cen-

BELOW:
The Getty Center,
Brentwood, California,
1997.

38

A Union of Technology and Humanity.

The theme of harmony in architecture expressed so often by Meier was also voiced by the 1987 Pritzker Laureate, Japan's Kenzo Tange. Tange, who designed some of the most outstanding buildings of the twentieth century, received the award when he was 74 years old, and had a major influence on many significant architects of the century who studied under him, including Arata Isozaki and Fumihiko Maki, who went on to win the Pritzker several years later. The Pritzker panel applauded Tange's efforts by stating that, "In preparing a design, Tange arrives at shapes that lift our hearts because they seem to emerge from some ancient and dimly remembered past and yet are breathtakingly of today." And Maki notes that his mentor has "an ability to distill the very essence of the modern spirit . . . wedded to a deep understanding of traditional Japanese culture." But perhaps Tange explains his exciting and beautiful work best: "Architecture must have something that appeals to the human heart, but even then, basic forms, spaces and appearances must be logical. Creative work is expressed in our time as a union of technology and humanity."[7]

ter, conservation institute and a collection of gardens. Many consider it to be the most significant commission of the twentieth century, and most will agree that it has become Meier's masterpiece. Using a handful of his signature materials — metal, glass and stone — he has managed "to create a work of art/architecture that excites visitors as much as the art collection inside."[8] The stunning travertine stone from the south of Italy complements the surrounding gardens. Bathed in light as it sits atop the hill, the rich stone creates a stunning image and thoroughly satisfying artistic experience for visitors, whether they are inside or outside the structures, on the campus or looking up at it from the surrounding area.

Meier continues to innovate and amaze, proving, as he did recently with the Perry Street Towers project in New York City, that a residential apartment tower "need not use the routine materials, construction methods and rectilinear form that defines so many of their midtown cousins."[9] This pair of minimalist transparent towers overlooking the Hudson River has become one of the most sought after

39

addresses in Manhattan for those looking for a cool modernist perch. The structures are a sensational celebration of light and space, sheathed in volumes of
clear blue glass, natural concrete and Meier's signature white aluminum bands.

"White is the most wonderful color," he explained in his Pritzker Prize
acceptance speech, "because within it you can see *all* the colors of the rainbow. For me, in fact, it is the color which in natural light reflects and intensi-
fies the perception of all of the shades of the rainbow, the colors which are

40

Gardens in the air.

Creativity takes many forms. Gordon Bunshaft, co-Laureate of the Pritzker in 1988, is acknowledged as opening a new era in skyscraper design with the New York commission for the Lever House. Bunshaft, like Richard Meier, has worked on numerous public projects, including some of the buildings for the 1939 World's Fair in New York. Aware of the art in architecture, Bunshaft described his design of loggias for the National Commerce Bank in Jeddah, Saudi Arabia, as "gardens in the air."

Co-Laureate in the same year, Brazilian Oscar Niemeyer was chief architect of Brasilia for many years before his retirement. He once expressed a desire to instill in young architects "the sensitivity to aesthetics . . . to strive for beauty in the manipulation of architectural form." To those who criticized his work, Niemeyer said, "My work proceeded, indifferent to the unavoidable criticism set forth by those who take the trouble to examine the minimum details, so very true of what mediocrity is capable of." He went on, "It was enough to think of Le Corbusier saying to me once while standing on the ramp of the Congress: `There is invention here'."

But few would now use the name "Niemeyer" and the word "mediocre" in the same breath — so significant have been his contributions to the world of art and architecture. If he had done nothing more than his major masterpiece, Brasilia, the capital of Brazil, he would still be revered. He went on, however, to create an immense and important body of work, including one of the most significant structures in the world, the United Nations Headquarters, designed in collaboration with his one-time mentor, Le Corbusier.

constantly changing in nature, for the whiteness of white is never just white; it is almost always transformed by light and that which is changing: the sky, the clouds, the sun and the moon . . . In this way whiteness has been one means of sharpening perception and heightening the power of visual form."

As the Pritzker jury noted when presenting Meier his award, "what he has achieved is only prologue to the compelling new experiences we anticipate from his drawing board." He has proven to all that his white drawing board continues to be an incredibly versatile, multi-dimensional, and prolific tool. ■

"Man, there's another freedom out there, and it comes from somewhere else, and that somewhere else is the place I'm interested in."

— Frank Gehry[1]

CHAPTER 4

The "Other" Frank

Frank Gehry (1929-   )
1989 Laureate

In sharp contrast to the muted elegance of Richard Meier's buildings come the untamed, wild, and provocative 'deconstructionist' works of Frank Gehry, the Pritzker's 1989 Laureate. His works have been considered impossible to build. They have been called everything from "an architectural epiphany" to a "lunar lander in search of its moon."[2] They have glamorized industrial materials such as chain link fence and corrugated metal, which had never before been considered fit for building decoration and adornment. In the process, his work has energized and inspired a generation of architects, students, art lovers and even the uninitiated who are typically indifferent to architecture.

Wherever a Gehry building is found, there are likely to be tourists, sightseers, students and other curious souls. His work has matured and evolved over the years, with each new stage of development more exciting and original than the next. Yet, his older work still stands the test of time.

Since the Guggenheim Museum in Bilbao, Spain was unveiled in 1997, so dizzying has the pace and scope of his work been that the it's hard to believe he had already received his profession's highest honor — the Pritzker — so many years earlier. With the completion of recent projects like the Walt Disney Concert Hall in Los Angeles, the explosive music pavilion in Chicago and the "leaning towers" of the new science center on the conservative MIT campus, it's fair to say he's entered yet another phase of invention and creativity that's sure to quash any criticisms that he's stuck in a "son of Bilbao" sameness.

His enormous popularity and well-earned acclaim make it hard to believe that he ever had a struggle to gain recognition, but it took several decades of quiet contemplation and sheer innovation for Gehry to first find success. So startling and intensely unusual was Gehry's early work that he was initially snubbed by his fellow architects and found more support and encouragement among the artist community. He befriended and collaborated with abstract artists and sculptors like Jasper Johns, Robert Rauschenberg, Richard Serra, Ed Moses and Claes Oldenburg, who rose from obscurity to prominence along with him. He was "intellectually intrigued with their process, their language, their attitudes and their ability to make things with their own hands." Among his fellow architects — he felt more like "an outsider."[3]

The art of architecture . . .

"Architecture must solve complex problems. We must understand and use technology, we must create buildings which are safe and dry, respectful of context and neighbors, and face all the myriad of issues of social responsibility, and even please the client.

But then what? The moment of truth, the composition of elements, the selection of forms, scale, materials, color, finally, all the same issues facing the painter and the sculptor. Architecture is surely an art, and those who practice the art of architecture are surely architects."[4]

But today he is very much an insider. He's an A+ list architect, always in demand, much sought-after. He is in the unique position of turning plum commissions down, which he does if the client is not in sync with his adventurous spirit or artistic approach.

His stature has changed from outsider to pop culture icon, and it's easy to understand why. He is a complete original. He manages to explore classical architecture themes and express them in an exploding deconstructive aesthetic. And out of all the chaos, he's managed to create wonderful, inviting, serene spaces. Above all, he has managed to get people excited about architecture — even passionate about it.

It's no wonder that comparisons to "the other Frank" have begun. They are, of course, referring to the American master Frank Lloyd Wright. It is said that Gehry has now designed "the other Guggenheim," the one in Bilbao, Spain rather than the Wright original in Manhattan. They are both big risk-takers. Like Wright before him, Gehry is credited with inspiring a new generation of

45

architecture students, giving them a different way to see, think and create. He's designed furniture, as did Wright, and it is said that he is fast gaining household-name status, along with Wright.

But why draw comparisons? They are both pure geniuses, and the Pritzker jury recognized this quality in Gehry years before he had even started to reach his full potential. As they noted in their closing statement, though the award is a for a *lifetime* achievement, in his case it was for a "work in progress."

"He builds," says Pritzker juror Ada Louise Huxtable, "on the liberated 'box' that Frank Lloyd Wright broke open forever, and liberates the spaces that Le Corbusier raised to luminous heights . . . He pushes the modern miracle of radically redefined structure and space into sudden bursts of pure form — a surprising exterior stair, a sky-lit room that offers as much abstract art as illumination . . . He will continue to work at the less-than-easy edges, turning the practical into the lyrical, and architecture into art."[5]

Frank Gehry's early years were fairly unremarkable, and presaged nothing of his future celebrity. Born in Canada in 1929, the young Gehry "spent his childhood making little cities out of woodscrap"[6] and drawing. While

in his teens, the family moved to Los Angeles and he earned his architecture degree from the University of Southern California in 1954. He moved to Paris with his wife and children in 1961, then back to Southern California.

It wasn't until 1978, after practicing for more than 20 years, that he finally received national attention for his work. Ironically, it was for an inexpensive renovation of his own Santa Monica house. He took his modest little bungalow and modified it with an unheard of combination of industrial materials: Corrugated sheet metal, exposed tilted wood-frame supports, concrete blocks, chain link fence. He even covered the kitchen floor in asphalt. This was the far edge of cutting-edge back then, which has since become almost middlebrow. Years later — and van loads of students and tourists later — the house remains a popular destination for those hoping to catch a glimpse of where this super-star architect started it all.

The decades since have produced an astounding body of breathtaking buildings, all "jutting, unusual shapes juxtaposed with simple geometric forms," wildly curving metal-clad buildings and leaning towers. There's the Raisin Building in Prague, more widely known as "Ginger and Fred" as it dances around the corner like the famous couple. There's the energetic Experience Music Project in Seattle, Washington (2000), commissioned by Microsoft co-founder Paul Allen and dedicated to the memory of Jimi Hendrix. There's the Vitra Design Museum in Weil-am-Rhein, Germany, the "Fish" in Barcelona, the Weisman Museum of Art in Minneapolis, the Chiat/Day "sculpture within a sculpture" office building with the eye-catching binocular sculpture, conceived in collaboration with sculptor Claes Oldenburg. There's "temporary" Contemporary Museum of Art in Los Angeles, designed to be a temporary space while the new museum was built, but so beloved by art lovers that it continues to hold exhibits. There are many small, innovative projects in and around Venice Beach, California, and the list can go on and

"I think my best skill as an architect is the achievement of hand-to-eye coordination; I am able to transfer a sketch into a model into the building."

— Frank Gehry

The Guggenheim Museum demonstrates Gehry's genius of design that arises from inspiration rather than from simple two-dimensional scale.

The creative process . . .

"My artist friends . . . were working with very inexpensive materials — broken wood and paper, and they were making beauty. These were not superficial details, they were direct. It raised the question of what was beautiful. I chose to use the craft available, and to work with craftsmen and make a virtue out of their limitations.

Painting had an immediacy which I craved for architecture. I explored the processes of raw construction materials to try giving feeling and spirit to form. In trying to find the essence of my own expression, I fantasized the artist standing before the white canvas deciding what was the first move. I called it the moment of truth."[7]

OPPOSITE PAGE:
Guggenheim Museum,
Bilbao, Spain, 1997.

on. Each bears his unique stamp as a work of art, architecture, and simple functionality.

However, it was the titanium masterpiece — the Guggenheim Museum of Bilbao, Spain — that has ingrained his reputation as one of the greatest architects of all time, and prompted the comparison to "the other Frank." Conceived from "wildly gestural sketches" and unlike rigid, engineered plans typically associated with architects, it demonstrates Gehry's genius of design that arises from inspiration rather than from simple two-dimensional scale. Though the museum has its detractors, the millions of visitors who have thronged through its doors since they have opened have joined the loud chorus of critics who have hailed it as one of the best buildings ever designed. It's been touted as "a building of such brilliant innovation and aesthetic triumph that it has been called a twentieth century Chartres."[8] And the "Dean of Architects," Philip Johnson quipped, "When a building is as good as that one, f..k the art!"[9]

The Walt Disney Concert Hall in Los Angeles opened in 2003 to huge critical acclaim as well, after more than a decade and a half in development. Gehry has dryly called it "his first major project in his hometown." Though begun well before the Guggenheim came to fruition, and completed years after, many prejudged it by slinging "Bilbao effect" pot shots and comparisons. For the most part, however, the critics were silenced when Maestro Esa-Pekka Salonen raised his baton and heard the first notes played. He is said to have cried, so glorious was

ABOVE:
Walt Disney Concert Hall,
Los Angeles, California,
2003.

the sound. And as for the building itself, "from the stainless steel curves of its striking exterior to the state-of-the art acoustics of the hardwood-paneled main auditorium,"[10] it is not only acoustically stunning, it's visually exciting and has already achieved must-see landmark status. Paul Goldberger describes it as a "Serene, ennobling, building" that will give the people of Los Angeles — known as a "city of private places, a new sense of the pleasures of public space."[11]

So where does he stop? It's unlikely we'll know for quite some time as each year he continues to surprise and amaze, rolling out project after project that literally can take the breath away. They're structures like no others, and it's hard to even begin to understand where they've come from. "He pushed the modern miracle of radically redefined structure and space into sudden bursts of 'pure' form." And he doesn't slow down.

He's also designing everything from a new Vodka bottle to watches for the Fossil Company. Why? "I am always attracted to things that are a challenge." More to the point, "It's a quick fix. Architecture takes so long. That's why you do the small stuff — instant gratification."[12]

After winning nearly every major architecture award and continuing to dazzle, it's hard to know where he'll go next. And with Gehry, that's half the fun. You know it will be somewhere no architect has tried to go before. As Karen Templer wrote for Salon.com: *Frank O. Gehry: The Complete Works* was recently released, and it seems as highly premature as was his lifetime achievement award from the Pritzker people."[13] With a "mile-long list of projects in the hopper . . . a new stacking chair for Knoll, a new wing for the Corcoran Gallery of Art, which he said looks like a bunch of colored pieces of paper and more . . . there's no reason to believe, when all is said and done, his Guggenheim will stand out as his masterwork."[14]

In his Pritzker Prize acceptance speech Gehry said, "Former laureates have gone on to do magnificent projects, and that is the challenge, to do better and finally bring great honor to this prize. That is what I intend to do." And though he's already succeeded, it's what he continues to strive for. ■

Gehry on Shapes . . .

INTERVIEW: "Why these shapes? Why do you twist and turn like that? Why would anybody do that?"

GEHRY: "It has to do with my belief that a building can have feeling. That there can be buildings that are deadly inert and don't give you anything. My favorite buildings, you either hate 'em or you love 'em. You get emotional. You can go into great buildings and they evoke some kind of an emotion and a lot of modern architecture is deadly and doesn't."[15]

51

"At the moment . . . the need and the way to add quality to things that are banal and repetitive . . . as a condition to enhance the beauty of the city . . . is facing profound transformations. . . . The aim of an architectural prize is supposed to be, above all, that of celebrating perfection.

I have not yet been able to reach perfection."

— Álvaro Siza

CHAPTER 5

Deceptive Simplicity

Álvaro Siza (1933-   )
1992 Laureate

Frank Gehry has, undoubtedly, made his mark on contemporary architecture in bold, dramatic strokes. And to achieve his explosive results, he has used modern technology and materials in ways that had never been considered before and have since, literally changed the way modern architecture is perceived and practiced. However, his work has not precluded others from continuing to practice a softer, gentler type of architecture and in 1992, the Pritzker Prize was awarded to a much more subdued and sensual type of artist — Portugal's best-known architect, Álvaro Siza.

The Pritzker jury described Siza's enigmatic work as "a joy to the senses," claiming his architecture "uplifts the spirit." Another has characterized it as "the heroic spirit of modern architecture." Vittorio Gregotti, professor of architecture at the University of Venice, stated that "Álvaro Siza could be justifiably considered the father of the new architectural minimalism."[1] In fact, Siza's work, like the work of so many exceptional architects, cannot be easily labeled. The early Modernist movement unmistakably influenced his roots. But Siza's conviction that every detail must be a precise response to problem, and that it must be grounded in the topography and texture of the local fabric was the catalyst for ushering in a new development in Modern architecture that had a "regional" approach.

Building primarily in his native Portugal, Siza's sleek, modern structures were built in materials common to his area: bright white marble and granite on the exterior, crisp white stucco on the interiors which related perfectly to each site and to the area. By further manipulating the subtleties of local light, craftwork and materials, he created beautiful modern structures that also displayed a respect for "locational sensitivity," and at the same time conveyed a deceptive simplicity.

This "deceptive simplicity" is hard to explain. It's hard to describe and even hard to photograph, which is why so few photos of his work are available. But this quality is what ultimately charms all those who experience his work. It is what has made the architecture community rapturous over Siza, why he has received so many accolades and honors over the years. Ultimately, it is what earned him the top honor of his profession, the Pritzker Prize.

Siza was raised in Matosinhos, a small town on Portugal's northern coast, attended school at the University of Porto School of Architecture and eventually opened his own practice in Porto in 1955. He was also an instructor at the School of Architecture from 1966-1969. Over the years, most of his commissions have been in and around his native country. However, his constant experimentation, fresh approach, and painstaking attention to detail resulted in projects so exquisitely done that he quickly began to gain international acclaim for both his overall *approach* to architecture as well as the incredible *results* of his architecture.

Siza has said: "Every design is a rigorous attempt at capturing a concrete moment of a transitory image in all its nuances."[2] His explanation of the transitory quality of artistic expression and the visualization of the artistic process he goes through is one that all creative people can relate to. A musician might well use the same description of the process that goes into creating the audio imagery of music, much as an artist may use it to describe the visual and emotional components of painting. For Siza, every detail that goes into a project is more than an

Robert Venturi

It is important to mention the 1991 Pritzker Prize recipient Robert Venturi (1925-), who is known for his writings as much, as for his built work. He began his career working for two of the greatest twentieth century architects, Eero Saarinen and Louis I. Kahn. By 1958, he had formed his own practice, and his own unique views on architecture.

In sharp contrast to Álvaro Siza, Richard Meier and other International Style disciples, Robert Venturi rejected what he perceived to be the banality of modern architecture in favor of symbolically decorated architecture based on historical precedent. "Less is a bore," became his mantra, as he fought for what he called "the messy vitality of the built environment."[3] His theories on a need for a more contextual approach to design were outlined in his controversial book *Complexity and Contradiction* in Architecture (1966), which is widely considered to be responsible for ushering in the Post-Modern era and aesthetic in architecture.

Unlike the modernists, Venturi believes structure and decoration should be separate entities, and decoration should be a reflection of the times. His book *"Learning from Las Vegas,"* written with Stephen Izenour and his wife, Denise Scott-Brown, went further by glorifying strip malls and road signs, and accepting the "kitsch of high capitalism" as a form of vernacular architecture. An architect, scholar, author and teacher, Venturi's theories of symbolically decorated design based on precedents have since become highly debated in the architecture community.

The bold early work of Robert Venturi, such as the Guild House in Philadelphia (1966) — with it's big billboard-like entrance, have "given way to a more restrained historicizing mode found in later work like the Sainsbury Wing of the National Gallery, London (1991), and the expanded Museum of Contemporary Art, San Diego (1996)."[4]

Though his Post-modern principles remain somewhat heretical and continue to generate controversy, the Pritzker committee recognized him for "changing the course of architecture . . . allowing architects and consumers the freedom to accept inconsistencies in form and pattern, to enjoy popular taste."[5]

incident or a purely technical requirement. As Gregotti has noted, "nothing is planned in and of itself, but always in relation to belonging."

Put another way, the Pritzker jury citation said, "his shapes, molded by light . . . are honest. They solve design problems directly. If shade is needed, an overhanging plane is placed to provide it. If a view is desired, a window is made. Stairs,

"I have always had the impression that Álvaro Siza's architecture sprang from archaeological foundations known to him alone — signs invisible to anyone who has not studied the site in detail through drawings with steady, focused concentration."

—Vittorio Gregotti
Architect, Professor of Architecture, University of Venice, Italy

ramps, and walls all appear to be preordained in a Siza building. That simplicity, upon closer examination however, is revealed as great *complexity*. There is a subtle mastery underlying what appear to be natural creations. To paraphrase Siza's own words, his is a response to a problem . . . in which he participates."[6]

A number of Siza's most highly regarded structures, beginning with a swimming pool at Quinta de Conceicao Matosinhos completed in 1965, reflect this "deceptive simplicity" that has become such a hallmark of his work.

In 1977, Siza was commissioned to design a 1,200-unit housing project in Evora, Portugal called *Quinta da Malagueira*. His goal was to create a modern subdivision while also retaining harmony with the landscape of olive groves. The result appears disarmingly simple because his approach to it was more tactile and tectonic than visual. But it's a glorious fusion of references to the modern and the historic. His design included courtyards for all of the units, which were a mix of one-and-two-story homes, white-washed cubic forms with terraces, and innovative use of elevated bridges moving through the project to carry piping and services. By strategic and well-planned placement of a wall, a window, an empty space, a colored door within a vast stretch of plaster surfaces — he was able to create a magical, serene place. Of this project, Siza humbly observed that as an architect he did not *invent* anything; he merely worked with models as a response to the problems encountered. But his "simple" explanation belies his skillful artistry.

Another example of his "deceptive simplicity" is seen in the design for the Meteorology Center in Barcelona, Spain. This building, constructed of concrete and brick, looks like a simple closed cylinder but is an interesting study in spatial relationships and form fitted to environment. Eight separate openings in what appears to be a simple cylindrical expression become more complex upon examination. The shape opens up to expose a number of terraces and courtyards, and a central courtyard lets light into inner rooms. As usual, Siza made use of existing elements that serve to anchor the building to its surrounding area both in his choice of building materials and its location on the site.

Another of Siza's deceptively "simple" masterpieces is the Santa Maria Church in Marco de Canavezes, Portugal. Joining a larger complex of buildings, it was imperative that the new churches seamlessly blend into the pre-existing neighborhood. Siza's solution — with its soaring façade, two towers and ten-meter-high doors — could at first glance appear to be stern as well as simple. But his window placements allow natural light to flood in, while at the same time framing views of the surrounding mountains. Curves, ramps, and multi-levels connect rooms in provocative ways. The whitewashed walls and local materials — marble, wood, granite, tile — allow for local construction techniques to be used, thereby keeping costs in check. The overall effect prompted one writer to state, "Siza's signature is on every detail . . . Having read many articles about Santa Maria Church I was once again reminded that no graphic representation can adequately substitute for the direct visual and physical experience."[7]

Creating
unforgettable
scenes.

Fumihiko Maki was the 1993 Pritzker Laureate and like Álvaro Siza is associated with a "conscious effort to capture the spirit of a place." While using materials associated with the Modernist design movement — metal, concrete and glass — Maki has expanded his selections to include mosaic tile, anodized aluminum and stainless steel. "The problem of modernity," he has said, "is not creating forms, but rather, creating an overall image of life, not necessarily dominated by the concept of modernity." He favors the importance of human space and how it works, over the vision of a constructed façade. "In each building, he searches for a way to make transparency, translucency and opacity exist in total harmony. To echo his own words, "Detailing is what gives architecture its rhythm and scale . . . it is the responsibility of the architect to leave behind buildings that are assets to culture."[8]

The range of Siza's work has included innovative design in mass housing developments, apartment complexes, office buildings and a variety of commercial projects. Each project is a showcase of his sensitive, cultural approach to "regional architecture." This concept has gained Siza an international reputation and endeared him to his fellow architects who, perhaps, can best appreciate it. He has also made a conscious effort to remain new and original, as his playful bridge on the dynamic Vitra Design Center campus in Germany demonstrates.

"His architecture can communicate to us an extraordinary sense of freedom and freshness," as one article observed; "In it one clearly reads the unfolding of an authentic design adventure. In accepting the risks of such adventure, Álvaro Siza has even been able to bring to the surface, in his architecture, what one feared in danger of extinction: the heroic spirit of modern architecture."[9]

The Pritzker jury commented that Siza's designs reveal a simplicity that "upon closer examination . . . revealed great complexity. There is a subtle mastery underlying what appears to be natural creations." That same "deceptive simplicity" for which the Pritzker jury committee praised Siza is precisely what Siza himself

Glenn Murcutt

Another regional architect who has since gained international acclaim is the 2002 Pritzker Laureate, Australia's Glenn Murcutt. The Pritzker jury described his work as "a synthesis of Mies van der Rohe and the native Australian wood shed," and described him as "a modernist, a naturalist, an environmentalist, a humanist, an economist and ecologist." He "eschews large projects," they said, "which would require him to expand his practice, and give up the personal attention to detail he can now give to every project. His is an architecture of place, an architecture that responds to the landscape and to the climate." Like fellow regionalist Álvaro Siza, he uses materials from his native region, and puts emphasis on environmental sensitivity. "His structures float above the landscape," or, to quote an Aboriginal phrase from Western Australia, "they touch the earth lightly." Murcutt's ethic is guided by Henry David Thoreau's statement, "Since most of us spend our lives doing ordinary tasks, the most important thing is to carry them out extraordinarily well."

aspires to on every project. In his own words he has explained that, "what I appreciate and look for most in architecture is clarity . . . Simplicity results from the control of complexity and the contradictions of any program . . . The more character a building has, and the clearer its form, the more flexible its vocation."[10]

Perhaps Siza was right when he said that "architects invent nothing . . . they transform in response to the problems they encounter." Over many decades, Siza has been beautifully transforming the built environment by incorporating his pure and personal modernist vision to a varied architecture, and by showing deference and respect to his mission. He has combined respect for the traditions and materials of his native Portugal with respect for the context in which he is bound to create, whether it's an "older building, or the rocky edge of the ocean," along with an abiding respect for the unique challenges architects face working today.

As the Pritzker jury so eloquently put it, "his enrichment of the world's architectural vocabulary and inventory over the decades provides ample justification" for the many accolades and awards he has received over the decades — including the prestigious Pritzker Prize. ■

"In [a] world of rapidly transforming values, my hope is to help promote both an architecture and a city which can embrace humanity with enduring care and love."

— Tadao Ando

CHAPTER 6

Places of Serene Possibility

Tadao Ando (1941-   )
1995 Laureate

While Álvaro Siza was hailed as the "father of the new architectural minimalism," whose work reflected a marriage of traditional Portuguese roots with modern methods, an interesting parallel can be seen three years later when the Pritzker Prize was awarded to Tadao Ando of Japan. Ando also blends Modern techniques with regional mores, which in his case are found in traditional Japanese aesthetics and reserve. The result has been a series of sensitive, beautifully crafted and original structures that first won the praise of his fellow architects and then the respect and admiration of the world. His work has earned him virtually every major international architecture award, including the world-renowned Pritzker Prize in 1995.

And while Ando's work is clearly a mix of modern and Japanese architectural styles, he possesses what the Pritzker Jury called an "inner vision" that guides him to create buildings that are unique and inspiring at every turn and defy categorization or class. As the jury noted, "Tadao Ando is that rare architect who combines artistic and intellectual sensitivity in a single individual capable of producing buildings, large and small, that both serve and inspire. His powerful inner vision ignores whatever movements, schools or styles that might be current, creating buildings with form and composition related to the kind of life that will be lived there."[1]

One of the most remarkable aspects of Ando's career is that he is completely self-taught and received no formal training or architecture education. Instead, he learned his craft on his own by reading books, by visiting the key temples, shrines, tea houses, and museums in his country, by traveling abroad, by apprenticing with craftsmen, and sketching it all as he went. It is even more remarkable that, despite his lack of professional training, the 35 buildings he designed and built in Kobe, Japan all survived the devastating 1995 earthquake that rocked the town. His self-taught program of architectural study and his "innate sensibilities for space, form, light and materials" have made Tadao Ando one of the most original and captivating artists to receive the Pritzker Prize.

As a young boy, Tadao Ando was fascinated with shapes, structures and the forms of nature. He spent his youth making wooden models of ships, airplanes and buildings — learning the craft from local carpenters and apprenticing with several designers and city planners. Everything from the way the trees grew, to how the sun hit and altered the quality of the lumber, intrigued the young Ando and left a deep mark on his inquisitive mind. In his late teens, he began traveling to prominent Japanese sites such as temples, shrines and other significant buildings, including Frank Lloyd Wright's Imperial Hotel, analyzing how they were crafted, tracing drawings and researching the buildings on his own. This was followed by visiting the great buildings of the western world in Europe and the United States where the influences of Le Corbusier, Mies van der Rohe, Alvar Aalto and other modernist icons took hold.

The result, in his own words, is that he "came to understand the absolute balance between a form and the material with which it is made." In 1969, at the age of 28, Ando opened his own practice in his home city of Osaka — Tadao Ando Architect and Associates — and from that point on, began a prodigious volume of work.

His first commissions focused primarily on residential work. The Rokko Housing project, begun in the 1980s and completed in phases over a number of years, is perhaps the most prominent residential project from this period, and still one of his most spectacular. This multi-family apartment community was built directly into the Kobe Mountain and provided spectacular views of Osaka Bay, thanks to Ando's deft implementation of a symmetrical plan that intentionally created gaps to ensure privacy for each unit. The unique Rokko design featured terraces facing varying directions, all staggered along a rugged slope overlooking the water. More significantly, it incorporated a variety of materials and design features that would come to be representative of his work over time. When viewed as a whole, Rokko represents a clear expression of Ando's use of simple geometric forms, his impeccable and precise craftsmanship, his strategic use of lighting, and the introduction of his signature building materials — pure, clean concrete, steel and glass. All are in complete and perfect harmony with their natural environment

This beautifully executed project garnered Ando Japan's top architecture prize in 1986, and it became an excellent illustration of his personal design philosophy. As he puts it, "To think architecturally is not merely to deal with external conditions or to solve functional problems . . . We must create architectural spaces in which man can experience — as he does through poetry or music — surprise, discovery, intellectual stimulation, peace and the joy of life."[2]

Three other significant projects in Japan exemplify Ando's creative blend of traditional Japanese and contemporary Western design. Each employs his textural

"A key part of Ando's architectural philosophy is the creation of boundaries within which he can create introspective domains, encapsulating space where people can interrelate . . . away from the surrounding chaos."[3] —Bill Lacy, architect and director of the Pritzker Prize International Panel of Jurors

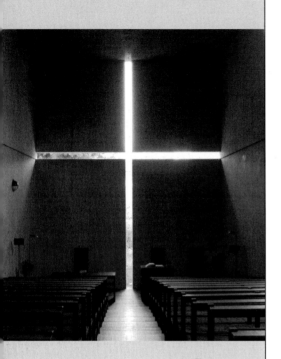

Tadao Ando created places of worship that are serene, meditative and elegant "with his mastery of space proportions, geometry and controlled light."

use of concrete, glass and steel, and his recurring themes of light, shadows, underground enclosures, geometric forms and spaces: The Church on the Water (Hokkaido, 1988); The Church of Light (Osaka, 1988), and Water Temple (Hyago, 1991).

All three are gorgeous concrete structures that feature surprise sloping and intersecting vertical and horizontal slits that let light peek through to subtly illuminate the sanctuaries. In each he employed highly polished concrete planes and platforms to express the Japanese concepts of *ma* (the spirit of place), *shakkei* (linkage of foreground and background), and *oku* (fusion between the natural and the artificial). All three use simple building materials in extraordinary ways. "From ordinary, monochromatic concrete, clear glass and his mastery of space proportions, geometry and controlled light,"[4] Tadao Ando created places of worship that are serene, meditative and elegant.

Ando's first building commission outside of Japan was the Vitra Conference Pavilion (1993) in Weil am Rheim, Germany. This understated building is "austere and elegantly proportioned [in] a deliberate contrast to the flamboyance of [Frank] Gehry's neighboring design museum."[5] The style of this structure is similar to that of the Pulitzer Foundation for the Arts, an Ando commission completed in 2001. Described as being "deceptively simple," as have so many of Ando's projects, he considers the building a place of possibility or mutual discovery. As he explained, "I see it as a creation of space to inspire visitors, and even expand their consciousness."[6] Constructed of cast-in-place, fine-finish reinforced concrete, with two rectangular sections, one ten feet taller than the other, the lower roof level has a glass pavilion and roof garden, and a reflecting pool lies in between the two wings.

Another prominent commission in the United States, and one of his many contemporary museum projects, is the Modern Art Museum of Fort Worth, Texas (2002), popularly called "The Modern." With over 53,000 square feet of gallery space, The Modern bears Ando's stamp from every aspect and angle, yet it is highly original. The spare entrance to the museum "masks what lies beyond." Enter, and you are transported to a magical space that creates an amazing interplay between the interior and exterior through the use of natural light and "dramatic vistas." A soothing two-acre pool reflects three gallery pavilions, constructed of exquisitely situated concrete walls. Sharply cantilevered concrete roofs provide shade to the building's exterior, usher natural light into the galleries and give the building a sculptural beauty. The huge Y-shaped columns that support the roof structure are also symbolic, representing "peace and restfulness amid the unrest in today's society."[7] A vast glass wall wraps around the pavilions and reflecting pool, which allows visitors to "circulate and relax, to glimpse the outside world of nature,"[8] which is derived from the *engawa*, or narrow passage in traditional Japanese architecture that signifies the transition from an indoor room to the exterior. Beyond the pavilions and reflecting pool, visible through the glass wall, lies a large garden and a panorama of the city itself, "inspiring both the calm of nature and the energy of

OPPOSITE PAGE:
The Church of Light
Osaka, Japan, 1988.

"Architecture delivers a place's memory to the present, and transmits it to the future. Architecture differentiates nature, and also integrates nature, through architecture, nature is reduced to its elements and then drawn into unity. Thus nature is architecturalized and mans confrontation with nature is refined."

65

the distant skyline."[9] It has been said that this building "heightens the senses as you move through space." The interplay of light and shadows, and the use of water and reflection pools harmonize together to ensure all who visit a unique and spiritual experience. It's even been described as "the essence of Haiku."

Despite Ando's perpetual use of the same materials — concrete, glass and steel; despite his use of the same architectural elements — pillar, wall and vault — and despite his singular mission to unify all his structures with nature, he keeps reinventing. No two buildings are the same, even though derived from similar elements. The "different combinations of these elements always prove exciting and dynamic," the Pritzker jury panel noted. "Ando's architecture," they went on, 'is an assemblage of artistically composed surprises in space and form. There is never a predictable moment as one moves through his buildings. He refuses to be bound by convention. Originality is his medium, his personal view of the world and his source of inspiration."[10]

Ando has described architecture as *Chohatsu suru hako*, or "the box that provokes." He explains: "I do not believe architecture should speak too much. It

"I believe that the way people live can be directed by architecture."

"For me the most satisfying thing is when architecture can do something to make people's lives better, to inspire them."[11]

"For me, architecture is the same as thinking."

should remain silent and let nature, in the guise of sunlight and wind, speak."[12] And whether designing museums, commercial buildings, factories, shopping centers, homes or places of worship, his structures continue to inspire and quietly stir through their sheer serene beauty. His buildings are not bold, dramatic statements in the vein of Frank Gehry, but precious, poetic experiences.

The Pritzker jury noted, in closing, that Tadao Ando is on a "self-imposed mission to restore the unity between house and nature" and to "embrace humanity." Although he feels his architecture should not speak too much, his gestures towards humanity literally speak volumes, evidenced by the fact that he donated his entire $100,000 Pritzker Prize monies to the orphans of the deadly earthquake that hit Kobe in 1995. It is a gesture that clearly speaks for itself and embodies the true spirit of the Pritzker Prize in its mission to honor an extraordinary talent that has made significant contributions to humanity through the art of architecture. ■

"Every building tells a different story. So the building is more important than you as an architect."[1]

— Renzo Piano

CHAPTER 7

A Magician — Rooted in the Believable

Renzo Piano (1937-   )
1998 Laureate

As we have seen with other Pritzker winners, many of the ground-breaking innovations they popularize quickly get adapted into the fabric of our daily life. Just as Philip Johnson's steel and glass towers have become the norm for corporate and urban centers, 1998 Laureate Renzo Piano's technological and engineering innovations — seemingly revolutionary when introduced to the architectural world — have since become mainstream.

The Italian born Renzo Piano is keenly identified with the onset of the Hi-Tech movement in architecture. However, he is celebrated for being far more than just a high-tech guru. He's a true artist and brings a humanistic touch to every project, always responding to the needs of the client and the individual site. Painstaking attention is given to workmanship and detailing, values he learned growing up amongst craftsmen in the family construction business. Although he is credited most with being a forward-looking practitioner who incorporates new technologies into his architecture, he continually draws from historical reference and his own personal past.

Renzo Piano has been remarkably prolific throughout his diversified career. In fact, so remarkable is his portfolio of projects that it is difficult to select just a few to highlight. He's progressed from stunning small-scale projects to mid-size museums, bridges, churches, cars and city-planning projects, on to such massive undertakings as the Kansai Air Terminal in Osaka Bay, Japan — until recently the largest and, arguably, most amazing airport in the world. All of his prodigious output has been handled with a marvelous mix of poetic sensitivity, industrial achievement and a head for putting art first. As Pritzker juror Ada Louise Huxtable noted: "Renzo Piano celebrates structure in a perfect union of technology and art."

His artistic and creative spirit has made him one of the world's most beloved modern architects, and a wonderful role model for all aspiring Pritzker Prize winners.

Born into a family of builders, Renzo Piano preferred to take a different path. He chose not merely to build, but create. He attended architecture school and upon graduation worked for a time in design for the family business, where he received his first significant commission in 1969 to design the Italian Industry Pavilion at Expo '70 in Osaka, Japan.

OPPOSITE PAGE:
Georges Pompidou Center
(also known as
Beaubourg), Paris,
France.

Through his involvement with the Expo, Piano met architect Richard Rogers. The two discovered they had much in common and they ended up entering and winning the international competition for the Georges Pompidou Center (also known as Beaubourg) in Paris. It turned out to be the project that made Piano's name one of the most recognizable in the world.

Located on a five-acre site in the heart of Paris, within walking distance from landmarks like Notre Dame and the Louvre, the Pompidou Center serves as a cultural complex with over a million square feet devoted to modern art, industrial design, literature and music. Another section provides space for retail outlets, offices, restaurants, theaters and parking. This vast cultural facility has been an enormous success over the years, averaging over 25,000 visitors per day. And the architecture has played a significant role in its appeal.

Renzo Piano Building of the
Centre Pompidou

"We had to make a structure out of pieces of cast metal. The entire French steel industry rose up in arms: it refused point-blank, saying that a structure like that wouldn't stay up. We were sure of our facts, and passed the order on to the German company Krupp. And so it was that the main structure of the Centre Pompidou was made in Germany, even if the girders had to be delivered at night, almost in secret. This was one case in which technique protected art. Our understanding of structures set free our capacity for expression."[2]

Designed in the new Hi-Tech school of architecture, the building was one of the first to take the hi-tech motif to such a massive scale. Meant to look like an "urban machine," the center is built of industrial elements and hard, shiny metallic surfaces. The most notable feature is that it exposes all of its engineering. Pipes, ducts, escalators, steel girders and other service elements actually become the façade. The shops, ticket sales, temporary exhibitions and other activities are revealed on the perimeter, while the gallery is one vast uninterrupted space on the interior forming almost a building-within-a-building effect. As one described it, "the building would be turned inside out, thus liberating the interior spaces from the permanent accommodation of circulation and servicing."[3]

What had always been hidden behind walls was suddenly now open to all. Rather than covering ducts and bracing materials, Piano's design glamorizes and accents them with brilliantly colored piping and service features. The result was a playful shock effect. And, while he had to fight long and hard to get his design completed precisely according to his plans, it ultimately became a triumph in innovation and a triumph in practical use. The exposed duct look has become popular and widely accepted in the decades since Piano popularized it, and the building continues to attract such massive volumes of visitors every year that significant renovations have since been required.

"He brings to each project a great seriousness of purpose, combined with a lyrical understanding of materials (and how they might come together)—so that what emerges is an architecture of extraordinary clarity and finesse."

—Charles Correa, Pritzker Juror

Like many artists who achieve celebrity early in a career, Piano had to overcome the stigma of being pigeon-holed as a hi-tech guru. He yearned to be seen as more than a maestro who produced a gigantic "folly" in Paris, and his future projects have gallantly succeeded in doing just that. As Paul Goldberger wrote in *Renzo Piano, Building and Projects 1971-1989*, "Renzo Piano has, in many ways, been more confined than liberated by the Centre Beaubourg, known primarily as the architect who installed this high-tech spoof at monumental scale in the heart of Paris."[4]

However, he *has* managed to move beyond this perception. His subsequent projects, from the 60,000-seat football stadium in Bari, Italy, to the controversial new London Bridge tower, all display "a light, tensile quality and an obvious love of technology. But where the expression of technology at Beaubourg was broad and more than a little satirical, in the buildings since Beaubourg, it has been straighter, quieter and vastly more inventive."[5]

The Menil Collection is a fine example

of how Piano uses technical sophistication on a sensitive, human scale. It is considered one of his greatest accomplishments and illustrates Piano's maturation process. Piano's program for this project, begun in 1981 and completed in 1986, was to create an open-air, naturally lighted art facility in a park setting, which also included an air-conditioned storage section for works not on display. Piano's concept was to create the effect of a museum "village" of sorts. The result was not only intimate and beautiful, but also sustainable, practical, and functional. The building is comprised of a thin steel frame which supports a complex aluminum superstructure. An amazing roof construction that contain a series of unique leaf-like ferro-concrete louvers filters solar heat and glare through a transparent glass ceiling.[6] The repeating modular "leaves" ingeniously function in sync as roof, ventilation and light control. Only cool light reaches the main hall, where exhibits are then viewed through natural light. The see-through effect brings the outside, inside, and more impressively, natural air conditioning and an abundance of naturally controlled light create serene, contemplative spaces.

The Menil was a structure ahead of its time. It also reaffirmed Piano's paradoxical mingle of hi-tech and humanistic concerns. As he noted, "the Menil Collection, with its great serenity, its calm, and its understatement, is far more 'modern,' scientifically speaking, than Beaubourg. The technological appearance of Beaubourg is parody. The technology used for the Menil Collection is even more advanced (in its structures, materials, systems of climate control), but it is not flaunted."[7]

Another building that is at once tranquil and reflective, yet environmentally and technologically advanced is the elegant Beyeler Foundation Museum near Basel, Switzerland (1997). Nestled among trees, one wall extends into the park forming almost a "green" entrance for visitors. The glass skin of the building is situated in layers that work to filter out electromagnetic light, maximize diffused light and prevent direct sunlight. The "transparent cantilevered roof of laminated glass augments the natural light and balances it with fluorescent fit-

Renzo Piano on
Transparency

"My insistence on transparency is often misunderstood and interpreted as insensitivity to the 'space' of architecture. In the jargon of our profession, to say that you have no sense of space is the vilest of insults. For many people, space does not exist except insofar as it is precisely—and solidly—circumscribed. This is a concept of space that disturbs me. It feels like the filling in a sandwich of bricks, a layer of air, squeezed between the walls that surround it. I have a less suffocating idea of space: the space of architecture is a microcosm, an inner landscape."

ABOVE:
Nasher Center,
Dallas, Texas.

tings. The result is an inviting glass box that is open and friendly to the surrounding nature yet, paradoxically, relies on ultra-sophisticated technology to prevent 98 percent of harmful solar radiation from penetrating displays. It is a brilliant combination of humanistic concern and industrial achievement, handled with the grace and beauty that has become Piano's signature.

"Technology cannot be an end into itself," noted Piano's former partner Richard Rogers. It "must aim at solving long term social and ecological problems." It's clear from the vast range of Piano's work that he employs technology as a tool to enhance the overall experience of the architecture. As the Pritzker jury chairman observed, "Piano's approach to design is always imaginative and inventive, technologically oriented, yet with the hand-crafter's attention to detail. His capacity for architectural problem-solving tempered by a poetic-sensibility has made possible his wide diversity of projects."[8]

"Renzo

Piano's command of technology is that of a true virtuoso; yet he never allows it to command him. Deeply imbued with a sense of materials and a craftsman's intuitive feel for what they can do, his architecture embodies a rare humanism."

—J. Carter Brown,
Pritzker Prize Jury Chairman

Piano succeeds to infuse massive, technically complicated projects with the same poetic sensibility seen in his more modest projects, as demonstrated by the Kansai Airport in Osaka, Japan (1994). It's one of the largest buildings ever built. The challenges were enormous. First, the site itself didn't even exist during the initial stages, as it was to sit on a man-made island in Osaka Bay. Second, it had to withstand rigorous earthquake and tidal wave regulations. And finally, it had to handle an enormous volume of traffic like a "precision instrument," no small feat for what was soon to become the world's largest airport.

True to form, Kansai was another triumph. Piano and his workshop team created a beautiful "structure with undulating, asymmetrical lines. It spread over the island like a glider . . . The planes determine form, function and extension." It blends in beautifully with its surroundings. It functions as mandated. It has withstood the shocks of an intense earthquake and registered "no damage, not even broken glass." Kansai became the "precision instrument," Piano envisioned, "a child of mathematics and technology."[9]

Perhaps Pritzker juror J. Carter Brown is more accurate when he called Piano, who was able to envision and execute this enormous project out of virtually thin air, "a magician, rooted in the believable."[10]

It would take volumes to list and describe Piano's significant body of work. From the remarkable curved glass hut-like structures of the Jean-Marie Tjibaou Cultural Center in New Caledonia (1998) to the huge Postdamer Platz reconstruction in the zone formerly dividing East and West Berlin, Germany, to the controversial London Bridge tower soon to soar above London's skyline, Piano has managed to make each project a work of art. Each possesses its own nuance, each a major technological challenge, yet all are brilliantly realized, with completely original resolution. Every project is approached on its own terms

Renzo Piano on Space

"The Gothic cathedral moves us with its spaces soaring into the sky, which draw the sinner's soul upward. It also stirs our feelings with elongated windows that shoot blades of light into the dark church, and by the colors that filter through the stained glass. We have to give our profession back its capacity to arouse the emotions by creating dramatic spaces, serene spaces, participatory spaces, secluded spaces. The choice is linked to the function and use of the setting.

If you are designing a museum, you offer contemplation. It is not enough for the light to be perfect. You also need calm, serenity, and even a voluptuous quality linked to contemplation of works of art."

rather than bringing a "Piano style" to it. And far from being confined by the early celebrity he enjoyed with the success of the Pompidou Center, he quickly allowed his imagination to take him to new and exciting places in his architecture, and the world's landscape has been the beneficiary.

The Pritzker citation applauded Renzo Piano's architecture as "that rare melding of art, architecture and engineering in a truly remarkable synthesis." It went a step further, likening his "intellectual curiosity and problem-solving techniques to earlier masters of his native land, Leonardo da Vinci and Michelangelo."

While those may be lofty comparisons to measure up to, it is clear that this Pritzker Prize recipient continues to fulfill the mission of the award by constantly reinventing, searching for new dimensions, and always managing to put art first.

He is, indeed, "a magician rooted in the believable." ■

"Ever since man came out of the cave, he has been on the cutting edge of technology, always pushing the limits. Technology is part of civilization . . . being anti-technology would be like declaring war on architecture and civilization itself."

— Sir Norman Foster[1]

CHAPTER 8

Romancing the Skyscraper

Sir Norman Foster (1935-   )
1999 Laureate

Renzo Piano's groundbreaking work on the Centre Pompidou, designed in partnership with Britain's Richard Rogers, is responsible for ushering in an era of High-Tech architecture. Many of the innovations they pioneered were soon adapted into the vernacular of everyday culture, due primarily to improvements in technology itself. The high-tech era proved to be a catalyst for cities to be built increasingly upward rather than outward. Buildings rose higher and higher as technology became more and more advanced. Sir Norman Foster, an early colleague of Richard Rogers, not only embraced high-tech but elevated it to heights many never dreamed possible.

In the same spirit of Pritzker Prize winners before him, Sir Norman Foster was never content to be a follower or imitator. A devoted student of the great architects, he applied their lessons to his own unique vision, personal beliefs and social concerns. He was one of the first to take an ecology-conscious approach to architecture and practice it on a grand scale. He went on to "set new standards for the interaction of buildings and their environment."[2] Likewise, he was one of the first to democratize the modern office and "restore a sense of community to the workplace" by adopting the open-plan model that later became the modern office standard.

But he is most associated with, and praised for, his treatment of the skyscraper — the most pervasive image on the landscape of modern cities. Our buildings have become ever taller and, at the same time, more impersonal, bland and increasingly insensitive to the spaces they occupy and the people who occupy them. Changing that reality, putting a human face on the structures and bringing "a fresh creativity and innovation to a building type long thought to have been fully investigated by other architects," became Sir Norman Foster's driving force, and his triumph.

He has re-envisioned the skyscraper and devised shapes and forms that have re-interpreted the way we see and experience the skyscraper. And with skyscrapers becoming an inevitable part of our urban landscape, he has endeavored to humanize them. In short, he's taken the standard skyscraper form of floors-stacked upon-floors and completely broken with tradition.

The Pritzker Jury
Praises Foster . . .

"He has mastered the art of integrating successfully the colossal gesture with the small detail. It is not surprising then, that his work has elicited indisputable popular appeal in spite of the reductive 'high tech' characterization with which the professional press has continuously labeled it."

"The jury has chosen an architect who cares passionately about the future of this planet, an avowed optimist with a firm belief in technological progress, but who also believes that architecture is about people and the quality of life. He makes buildings that will not only last, but will work for the people that use them, and in the process provide an uplifting experience."

The results have been a body of work so impressive and previously unimaginable that even the most traditional cities now anxiously wait for a Norman Foster building to go up.

The versatility of his design practice has been expanded to include a wide range of products, from door handles, to furniture, to a solar-powered bus and private yacht. But it is through his buildings that thousands experience his work on a daily basis and get to appreciate the unique contribution he has made to their daily experience. He has closed the gap "between the art and craft of architecture, and the machinery of industry," and showed that it *can be bridged, but only by dispensing with orthodox modernist dogma or standardization, handmade by robots.*"[3]

Like most of his fellow Pritzker Prize winners, Sir Norman Foster "transcends categorization. At whatever scale, from a glass elevator to an airport, his vision forges the materials of our age into a crystalline, lyrical purity that is highly personal, brilliantly functional, and . . . downright beautiful."[4]

"Sir Norman Foster's buildings," Pritzker Prize Executive Director Bill Lacy said, "set a standard for design excellence in the use of modern technology pushed to its artistic limits." He has, the Pritzker jury maintained, remained "steadfast to the devotion of architecture as an art form,"[5] — raising the standards of his profession to new heights, much as he's taken his beautiful buildings to daring new places.

As a teenager, Foster was fascinated by architecture, avidly studying the works of Frank Lloyd Wright and Le Corbusier and treasuring a book on the history of architecture by Frederick Gibberd.[6] With his blue-collar upbringing, however, a college education seemed unlikely.

Following army service and a string of odd jobs, he landed a position at an architectural firm in Manchester, England — in the contracts department. Thrilled to be amongst architects, even if in the contracts division, he was also incredibly awed by the architects in the firm, so much so that he could barely hold a conversation with them. One day, while chatting with one of the student apprentices, Foster asked his opinion of Frank Lloyd Wright. The apprentice replied, "I don't think I know him. Is he a student at the college?"[7] Foster was as astounded by the response and lack of recognition for one of his heroes, as he

was emboldened by it. It gave him the confidence to show a portfolio of his sketches to his boss, who then swiftly moved him to the drawing office. The rest is architectural history.

He attended architecture school in Manchester, won scholarships and competitions that provided foreign travel to see the architectural treasures of Europe, and eventually won a fellowship to the Yale School of Architecture. While there, he met 1981 Pritzker Prize winner Sir James Stirling, and a young Richard Rogers.

When he returned to England in 1962 he formed his first practice, called Team 4, with Rogers, and two sisters, Wendy and Georgie Cheesman. Team 4 did a number of "small, ecologically-concerned residential projects." But it was the huge Reliance Controls factory in Swindon, UK (1966) that generated international recognition. It was Foster's first steel building, and one of the earliest examples of the "use of lightweight construction and industrial components" that were at the heart of the high-tech phase. "The economic realities of the project dictated the need for speed and flexibility, forcing a change in our building methods,"[8] Foster explained. And the innovative result included linked pavilions and glass-walled courtyards, with movable walls beneath an umbrella-like roof.

Team 4 disbanded in 1967 and in 1968 Foster began a long collaboration with twentieth century icon, Buckminster Fuller, whose influence continues to inform Sir Norman's work to this day. "The thing about Bucky," Sir Norman noted, "was that he made you believe anything was possible."[9] And thus began a period of landmark buildings that have seen him make the impossible, possible.

The Willis Faber & Dumas headquarters in Ipswich, England (1974) was a "pioneering piece of social architecture." The owners of this insurance company with over 1200 employees set in a drab town landscape, wanted to establish a sense of "community" in the workplace. Foster responded with a daring curved-façade building wrapped in glass, which hugged the natural contour of the site and played off the light differently and dramatically from sunrise to sunset. It also "featured three open floors with lots of light space, a central atrium, a

"If I can get carried away with some passion about the poetry of light in one of my projects, then I can also, in the same vein, enjoy the poetry of the hydraulic engineering."[10]

— Sir Norman Foster

rooftop restaurant, and swimming pool"[11] accessible to employees and their families — all revolutionary features in an office tower in the 70s. In addition, he featured an open-office plan well before it became the norm.

Another breakthrough building was the IBM Pilot Head Office in Cosham, England, in which he broke with tradition and foreshadowed the future by uniting in one workplace both computers and personnel. However, it was the Hong Kong/Shanghai Banking Corporation (1979), looming 50 stories above the plaza level, that started his major re-interpretation of the skyscraper. This "cloud toucher" has been recognized as "one of the world's great 20th century monuments, a new step forward in the evolution of the skyscraper."[12]

To break up the monotony found in most towers, create a sense of identity among different departments working in the massive building, and bring natural light in wherever possible, Foster stratified the tower, delineating what he termed "villages in the sky."[13] By devising a series of trusses with suspended floors, he lifted the building up to create a large open space that has become a favorite picnic spot. He created a daylit atrium that lights up each floor from within, and breaks the building up into three vertical layers of differing heights, creating an incredible effect. While it cost more to build than any other building of its time, it is still considered one of the world's top modern monuments for its innovative design, sense of social responsibility and sheer beauty.

With each successive tower, his "design objectives are guided not only toward the overall beauty and function of a project, but for the well-being of those who will be using it. The Commerzbank in Frankfurt-am-Main, Germany (1997) was not only the tallest building in Europe when built, but the world's first ecological high-rise. The stunning triangular shaped building boasts nine four-storey-high greenhouse

Sir Norman Foster

gardens that can be seen from every office angle, and "all offices are naturally ventilated with opening windows."

Sir Norman's impact on the cityscapes and city living around the world is an extension of his dedication to "green architecture" and improving the living and working conditions of people by applying the "appropriate use of technology." Most of his projects, big or small, have been designed with this social dimension in mind.

Germany's breathtaking new Parliament building is a perfect example of his expert blend of brilliant engineering, social sensitivity and deference to history and site.

It is entirely energy self-sufficient. A stunning glass dome "rises out of the historic shell of the Reichstag" and works ecologically by "reflecting natural light deep into the heart of the chamber. It is part of the natural ventilation for the building and is powered by renewable sources of energy. At night, the whole thing works in reverse, rather like a lighthouse beacon, to signal the process of democracy at work." A spiral ramp allows the public a viewing platform to look down on the Parliament, further symbolizing the "power of the public above the politicians who are answerable to them."[14]

His ingenious plan for the Third London Airport in Stansted, England (1991) not only became a significant energy saver; it became a beautiful building to view. By abandoning the traditional design model and turning it upside down, he was able to reduce the amount of artificial lighting generated, which in turn typically generated a lot of heat and thus required more energy to cool. Instead, he eliminated the wasteful energy source with a lightweight, "umbrella-like" roof structure that "seems to float above the convergence of road, rail and air modes of transport." The handsome building also has the power to enlighten travelers and viewers alike. Sir Norman relates how a security guard, who was on duty the night the Queen opened the building, told him "he had been guarding buildings all his life, but that was the first time he realized that a building could be beautiful."[15] Stansted has since become a model for airports around the world, including his own design for the Hong Kong Airport. And this sincere, unscripted statement from the security guard reinforces the mission of Foster's practice, and proves that he's brilliantly succeeded at turning it into reality.

"No detail should be considered too small. The ends are always social—generated by people rather than the hardware of buildings."[16] —Sir Norman Foster

Perhaps no skyscraper has spawned so much debate as the funky Swiss Re Headquarters (2004). Reflecting the influence of his early mentor Buckminster Fuller, and set in London's financial district, it is often referred to as "the egg," "the Gherkin," or names unfit to print. It is instantly recognizable as it looms above the London skyline. The glass-covered obelisk, with its strident swirl pattern, is also an environmentally progressive structure. The design maximizes daylight and natural ventilation, thereby using half the energy typically required by an office tower. "Equally important," Foster notes, "is its improved working environment with better views for everyone . . . and set in a generous public plaza that encourages a lively mix of urban life with shops, cafes, and a restaurant."[17]

"Since its inception, more than thirty years ago," Foster has said, his studio "has been driven by the pursuit of design excellence, based on a belief that our surroundings directly influence the quality of our lives, whether in the workplace, at home or in the wide variety of public spaces in between."[18]

This pursuit has enriched lives wherever his work is found around the planet. It has helped make our increasingly chaotic cityscapes more sane and livable. And it has helped improve our overall quality of life. As the Pritzker citation said of Sir Norman, "His design objectives are guided not only toward the overall beauty and function of the project, but for the well-being of those people who will be the end-users. This social dimension to his work [makes] every effort to transform and improve the quality of light."[19]

In short, Sir Norman has set new standards for the interaction of buildings with their inhabitants, with the environment, and with art and culture. As he reaches ever higher, he lifts us all up with him. ■

ABOVE:
Swiss Re Headquarters,
London, England, 2004.

"Surprise, invention, thoughtfulness, tension, and tradition turned on its head. A Koolhaas building is where ideas and humanism meet."

— Ingrid Sischy, *Interview*

CHAPTER 9

A Complete Original

Rem Koolhaas (1944-   )
2000 Laureate

"It seems fitting," remarked Thomas J. Pritzker, president of The Hyatt Foundation, "that as we begin a new millennium, the jury should choose an architect that seems so in tune with the future."[1] With that announcement, the Pritzker Prize for the year 2000 was presented to the groundbreaking, free-thinking, free-form designing Dutch architect, Rem Koolhaas. He has been called a Modernist, a Deconstructivist, even a humanist. But his work, like that of many of his fellow Pritzker honorees, has defied classification. In fact, he's a complete original. He has also been recognized as much for his books and writings, as for his buildings. An iconoclastic rule-breaker from the start, Koolhaas is one whose creative energy and search for original solutions has earned him the respect of his peers as well as the Pritzker jury.

Though Koolhaas' work is heavily influenced by technology, like that of Foster, Piano, Gehry and others, his output is more governed by *ideas* — by thoughts, challenges and, most importantly, by discovering solutions. He's as affected by modern culture as he is by his unbound imagination. Consequently, his designs have pushed the limits in his own inimitable way.

Even his career path bears a unique stamp. He began as a journalist and film writer, only later taking up architecture. In 1978, after graduation from Cornell, he published his first book, *Delirious New York,* which has since become a classic treatise on architecture, urban living and society, and secured his reputation as one of the leading theorists and thinkers of his generation.

When he launched his own firm, the Office for Metropolitan Architecture (OMA), its mission was not that of a typical architecture practice but instead "dedicated to finding new synergies between architecture and contemporary culture."[2]

Koolhaas has carved a unique space for himself in the architecture world by combining his passions and disciplines, by following his own path, and by constantly looking ahead. Perceived as "an architect/philosopher/artist, Koolhaas has expanded, and continues to expand, our perceptions of cities and civilizations," claimed Pritzker Prize Executive Director Bill Lacy. And with his "restless mind, conceptual brilliance, and ability to make a building sing"[3] he continues to influence contemporary design and to fuse the world of art and architecture in an exciting new way.

In 1968, after working as a journalist, co-writing the film noir "The White Slave" and drafting an unproduced script for soft-porn king Russ Meyer,[4] Koolhaas went to architecture school. He landed in New York following graduate school and became fascinated by "the dynamics of the city." His observations on everything from "the culture of congestion, to density, to the 'architectural mutations' of the city were chronicled in his *Delirious New York: A Retroactive Manifesto for Manhattan*. The book was a huge sensation because of its "irreverent fusion of scholarship, design and polemics."[5]

In 1975, Koolhaas formed the Office for Metropolitan Architecture with several partners. The stated objective of OMA was "the definition of new types of relations, theoretical as well as practical, between architecture and the contemporary cultural situation."[6] The office entered a number of competitions but it wasn't until 1987, after his addition to the Dutch Parliament aroused tremendous interest, that Koolhaas got to construct his first building. That project, The Nether-

> ## "The Netherlands Dance
> ### Theater (1987) in The Hague was one of the first completed projects to garner critical acclaim for OMA. A foyer shared with an adjacent concert hall consists of three levels: the lowest slotted beneath the auditorium tiers, above it a half-moon balcony, and at the top, a 'floating skybar.'"
>
> — ArchitectureWeek No. 157

lands Dance Theatre in The Hague, was described as "Eclectic Modern" and, because of its top-level floating skybar, it has been called one of nine "top buildings of the 20th century."[7]

From this point on, Koolhaas was launched on a remarkable roll that has "seen his built works, projects, plans, exhibitions and studies resonate throughout the professional and academic landscape, becoming a lighting rod for both criticism and praise."[8]

Since then, his body of work, like his Dance Theatre, has been an eclectic mix. With irreverent, avant-garde work for commercial clients as diverse as Disney, Prada, Conde Nast magazines, and the European Union, he is equally well known for small, sensitive projects such as the Maison a Bordeaux in Lille, France (1998). The client, in this case, had been in an auto accident and was confined to a wheelchair. He told Koolhaas, "I want a complex house because it will define my world." Koolhaas designed a remarkable three-level residence containing a nearly invisible glass room that is also a vertically moving platform, thus allowing the room to also function as an elevator and giving him access to the other two levels. "Had he *only* done the Bordeaux project, his niche in the history of architecture would have been secure," the Pritzker jury noted. His compassionate solution for this house was recognized by *Time* which named it the Best Design of 1998.[10]

His second book, *S, M, L, XL,* published in 1998 and co-authored by the provocative graphic designer Bruce Mau, further propelled him to cult figure status. This mind-bending collage of freewheeling essays, diary excerpts, photographs, architectural plans, sketches, cartoons, fables and parables intended to shake modern architects out of conventional thinking," has become the coffee table book for the ultra-hip, MTV generation.

In the years since, his practice has moved from the theoretical realm to the real as the number of exciting new commissions has started to stack up. One of the most interesting is The McCormick Tribune Campus Center (2004) on the grounds of the Illinois Institute of Technology in Chicago. On a campus originally designed by the revered Mies van der Rohe, and which bears his mark at every turn, designing *anything* would intimidate most architects. But Koolhaas was definitely up to the task and created a building that one visitor described as "destined for architectural glory."

The Impact of Journalism on His Architecture

"It influences everything in the sense that the driving force of journalism is curiosity, and a journalist has to capture in a relatively short time the intricacies of something he doesn't really know a lot about. In some ways, architecture is really similar. You have to conceptualize what the essence of something is in a relatively short time."[9]

— Rem Koolhaas

ABOVE:
The McCormick
Tribune Campus Center,
Chicago, Illinois, 2004.

Both fanciful and functional, Koolhaas devised a brilliant solution to one of the major site challenges. The elevated train tracks slice through the campus, dividing the residential grounds from the main campus buildings. "The railway has a huge impact on IIT's character," explains Koolhaas. "To proclaim a new beginning, we enclosed the section above the campus center in an acoustically isolating stainless steel tube, releasing the potential of the land surrounding it."[11] The Campus Center, thus, has two primary components: the one-story building that houses all the student functions, including the university bookstore and large computer room, and the giant elliptical tube that sits on top of building, muffling the roar of passing trains from the structure below.

Departing from the other proposals that primarily presented traditional stacked towers with glass that kept the noise to a minimum, Koolhaas' design ebulliently captures the spirit of the students, and has reinvigorated the weary campus.

93

"The Tube's slanting concrete supports and flaming orange top serve as a symbol of the renewed campus — the new IIT student Internet portal even calls itself "The Tube."[12] Rather than being intimidated by the prospect of designing on Mies' hallowed grounds, Koolhaas' design pays homage to him, while providing an exuberant space everyone wants to be in. In contrast to Mies' "less is more" philosophy, it could be said that for Koolhaas, "more is more, and a whole lot more is better still."[13]

Koolhaas has since been busy at work on three new projects that many feel could be his crowning achievements. All have been challenging to him and his studio, and each is redefining the urban landscape in exciting new ways. The first is an enormous skyscraper project in Beijing for Chinese state TV that is assuming "the self-consciously unskyscraper-like form of a giant loop" and has become an "exercise in extreme engineering and icon-mongering."[14] With a straightforward need to house the 10,000 plus CCTV employees, the building transcends the "predictable two-dimensional tower soaring skyward" by producing an exciting three-dimensional experience. It's visually arresting and definitely not your standard skyscraper.

The "shoe-box" shape Casa da Musica concert hall in Porto, Portugal presented a challenge of a different nature. At issue, was "how to escape from the tyranny of the notorious 'shoe-box' that remains, for the specialists . . . the best guarantee for perfect acoustics."[15] The final result retains the shoebox form that assures quality acoustics but also includes a huge window cut-out in the auditorium that overlooks the city, and a series of "voids" cut into the concrete exterior where other programs are held, and which make the building as interesting from the outside as it is functional within.

The third recent project, one of his few in the United States, has been garnering the most praise. "Seattle's magnificent new Central Library . . . is the most important new library to be built in a generation, and the most exhilarating," Paul Goldberger wrote in *The New Yorker*.[16] Herbert Mushchamp, the *New York Times'* venerable architecture critic, declared that it was "not just the most striking library in the past 30 years, but the most exciting new building it

Koolhaas on capitalism
and architecture

"With the triumph of capitalism, architects increasingly serve a moneyed elite rather than society as a whole. Yet most of the profession continues with the nostalgic pretence that it can make a difference. Because of the idolatry of the market economy in the past 20 years there is something fundamental happening to the status of the architect. Thirty years ago we could pretend to serve the common interest. I think that if you look at what we are doing, very few of us can claim that anymore. We are serving at best an enlightened private entity.

"But architects have never been the main authors of cities. And to the extent that they are, they have only been able to do that in the case of extreme authoritarian systems. And that is a fantastic paradox or tragedy of the architect, that our better impulses are connected to the utopian, but the utopian only works when connected to power."[17]

ABOVE:
Seattle Central Library.

has been my honor to review." And the *Seattle Times* said the "library defies accurate description. Just go, and prepare to be blown away."[18]

With this spectacular achievement, Koolhaas has once again proven that he is not just interested in creating incredible spaces or dazzling buildings. The project must *work*; it must achieve specific needs, and the Central Library (2004) is being praised for hitting the mark on every count. The exterior is a dazzling "Rubik's Cube" grid of mesh, steel and glass. The interior is sheer innovation. Gone are the book stacks which have long been at the heart of libraries. Instead, Koolhass invented the "books spiral" "which makes the library's collection open and accessible, and is designed to accommodate growth." Chartreuse-colored escalators and stairs slice through ramped floors, taking visitors from the "spirals" to the magnificent reading room, or to the computer room, which

On Koolhaas . . .

"Koolhaas may now be much in demand, but what makes him someone to watch closely is what he demands of architecture."[19]

Koolhaas has renamed "The Mixing Chamber." Topics are broken down into sections he's dubbed "Programmatic Clusters." But apart from the new vocabulary he's coined and the visual stimulation, the library actually *works*. It's easy to use and has a clear logic to it. "It emphasizes the value culture places on literacy. It makes you feel like you're engaged in a serious pursuit."[20] Koolhaas is being praised for reinterpreting and reinventing the library for a new generation. But, as Goldberger claims, his real achievement may be in *reaffirming it.*"

The buzz is that these projects could well be his defining buildings. But that's selling this talented provocateur short. His best work, no doubt, is yet to come. It is sure to be prompted, as before, by his new ideas, writings, theories and musings on popular culture. *Content*, his latest exhibition and book of the same name, is certain to stir up the pot of architectural/cultural discourse once again, as he proclaims his "manifesto for the new millennium." It also signifies a new phase for Koolhaas since, for the first time, "the rhetoric is matched by a significant body of real — as opposed to theoretical or unrealized — projects."[21]

Since receiving the 2000 Pritzker Prize, Koolhaas has virtually gone into overdrive, inventing new language, new typology, new ways of shopping, of thinking, and of seeing. His restless mind refuses to rest, and he's become "architecture's most prolific, influential and extreme oracle. While other architects have based their careers on a handful ideas, he has spawned thousands."

The new millennium will no doubt be the feeding ground for thousands more. ■

"There are

360 degrees,

so why

stick

to one?"

— Zaha Hadid[1]

CHAPTER 10

A Mandate of Unpredictability

Zaha Hadid (1950-   )
2004 Laureate

As we saw when Rem Koolhaas received the Pritzker Prize in 2000, the Pritzker jury had consciously chosen to begin the century with an architect they felt was keenly in tune with the future. Four years later, they continued their march into the future and away from the safe choices of the past. In fact, the 2004 Pritzker Prize Laureate may well become one of the most remembered in history.

Iraqi-born Briton, Zaha Hadid, became the first woman ever to receive the coveted prize. The Pritzker jury called Hadid one of the most gifted practitioners of the art of architecture, complimenting her "consistently original and strong personal vision that has changed the way we see and experience space. [Her] fragmented geometry," they noted, "and fluid mobility do more than create an abstract, dynamic beauty; this is a body of work that explores and expresses the world we live in."[2]

But the 2004 selection was not just groundbreaking in its choice of a female; it was controversial at the same time. For while Hadid's architecture has been highly respected for pushing the boundaries of design during the past two decades, her body of *built* work was meager in comparison with many of her predecessors. In fact, Christopher Hawthorne, writing in *Slate*, observed that until five years prior to receiving the Pritzker award Hadid's "only finished building was a small fire station in Germany."[3]

The question buzzing around architecture circles was two-fold: Could an architect with such obvious talent and promise, but only a modest portfolio of built product, actually qualify and deserve an award typically bestowed in recognition of a life-time of achievement? And more interestingly, why *would* such an immense talent *have* so little built inventory? The answers to both are complex and even somewhat subjective.

In selecting Hadid as the 2004 honoree, the jury chose to recognize Hadid for more than just her body of built work. They've praised her for the contributions she's made to the art of architecture through her teaching posts, through exhibitions of drawings, paintings, and stage sets and through the many competitions she's entered — and won — that have resulted in "creating an architectural idiom like no other." They chose to recognize and honor both her endless source of originality, as well as the struggle to get things built that is a by-product of such breathtaking originality.

What architecture
means to Hadid

"It is fundamentally about shelter. At the same time, it should give you pleasure. When people go out on to the fields they are always amazed because of the flatness or the light falling on different mountains, and you can achieve that through architecture. You can create all these incredible spaces with not much difficulty. That's what we're there for. Inventors of space." [4]

The Pritzker panel acknowledged that Zaha Hadid's angular designs often defied comprehension and intimidated potential clients. But they chose to celebrate her talent and show their faith in her innate abilities, affirming that they believe she will go down as "one of the great architects of the 21st century."

Recognizing Hadid merely for being the first woman to receive the distinction would do her a huge disservice. The Pritzker committee carefully and cogently explained why Hadid is so deserving. They point to the quality rather than the quantity of her work to date and to the many prominent commissions she recently garnered. They point to the exciting work she currently has in progress. And more importantly, they point out that Hadid, like most of the 25 male predecessors, is actually destined to make her biggest contributions to the art of architecture in the years following her award. She is already well on her way.

Born in Baghdad in 1950, Zaha Hadid's formal education began at the Architectural Association in London, where she was awarded the school's Diploma Prize in 1977. Upon graduation, she worked for several years in the Office of Metropolitan Architecture, an avant-garde, boundary-pushing firm founded by fellow Pritzker Prize winner Rem Koolhaas. In 1979, she stepped out on her own, setting up a private practice in London.

For years, Hadid was best known as a theorist and had to be content with "small, albeit inventive, European commissions." Though her renderings and competition perspectives were critically acclaimed by her peers and broke daring new ground in their sheer innovation, few real-world decision makers were willing to take the leap of faith needed to construct them. Many simply feared her designs were just too unusual for their tastes, or those of their neighbors. Her designs, some felt, "made an enemy of aesthetic clarity and legibility."[5] With renderings that seemed to have been composed "from the perspective of a helicopter dipping into a crazy sideways tailspin,"[6] it's easy to understand why it was hard to get clients to open their minds — and pocket books — to her other-worldly designs. It's a fate that other pioneering architects, including fellow Pritzker recipient Frank Gehry, have experienced to lesser degrees along the way.

So, Hadid continued to teach, to draw, to enter competitions and to build precious, imaginative structures when risk-takers were willing to throw their faith in her favor.

101

One of her most recognized and praised projects — in fact her first built project — was the Vitra furniture factory's striking fire station in Weil am Rhein, Germany (1999). Set among a complex of groundbreaking buildings designed by a virtual "who's who" of contemporary architects, the firehouse "not only proved her talent, but launched her career as a legitimate, *building* architect."[7] Rather than be overshadowed or intimidated by the notion that her project would sit among a campus of buildings designed by architecture legends like (and Pritzker Prize recipients) Frank Gehry, Tadao Ando and Álvaro Siza — Zaha Hadid was empowered by it. She created a dramatic and seductive structure of alarming angles and audacious shapes. The inside was equally as imaginative, with a reckless use of angles and colors playing clever "tricks" on viewers. Walls and ceilings avoided 90-degree angles, slanting and sloping wildly, and stairs jutted out in odd configurations. Built as a working firehouse at the time, it now functions as a chair museum for the Vitra collection. But the building continues to captivate, drawing throngs of sightseers and students, and continuing to be considered one of the most astounding buildings built to date, and as intense as the drawings in many ways.[8]

If the Vitra Firehouse put Hadid on the map as a seriously ingenious architect, the attention-grabbing Bergisel Ski Jump tower she completed in Innsbruck, Austria (2002) furthered that reputation. Though the design has earned nicknames such as "cobra," "high-heeled shoe," and "golf club," her sweeping abstract design sits perfectly among the Alps and has, in short order, achieved landmark status. It also proved that her mind-bending conceptual drawings presented little problem in actually being brought to realization.

In 2002, Hadid won the AIA, UK Excellence in Design Award for a sweeping civic project she did outside of Strasbourg, France. The Terminus and Car Park in Hoenheim, essentially a city tram station, is a structure so stunning that it prompted one of the jurors to comment, "The more I look at it, the more perfect it gets."[9] This modest but magical structure is more than just a building or a traditional station house. Hadid translated the movement of cars, trams, bicycles and pedestrians into a constantly shifting whole. The parking lot, a space to hold 700 cars, also expresses the *idea* of the cars as a shifting, ephemeral element, a directional field of white lines on a black tarmac. The lines for each parking spot rotate with the site's curving boundary, thus creating reciprocity between static and dynamic elements in the design. Hadid's goal was to create a "new notion

that blurs the boundaries between natural and artificial environments,"[10] and she succeeded. With it's mélange of sloping concrete, glass and metal planes, it's a startling sight and one that takes public transit to an entirely new level by blending art, architecture and life.

As exhilarating as these structures have been, Hadid has continued to struggle to bring her dynamic and mesmerizing visions to fruition. Though respected by her peers and handful of bold clients, the timidity of potential clients has remained an issue. Pritzker jury chairman Lord Jacob Rothshild validates this view when he wrote; "Such are the forces of conservatism that, sadly, one cannot find one single building of hers in London."[11]

That predicament is bound to change soon. Hadid has recently enjoyed a spate of exciting new commissions, and the Pritzker Prize is certain to increase the volume of her built work, forever releasing her from the "cult of obscurity." Moreover, the newly opened Rosenthal Center for Contemporary Art in Cincinnati, Ohio (2004) — her first building in the United States — is sure to change her fate and cement her reputation as, to quote Pritzker juror Ada Louise Huxtable, "one of the most gifted practitioners of the art of architecture today."

The Rosenthal Museum is being hailed a triumph, and a window into a more complex, sophisticated Hadid. Missing are the phalanx of slashing planes and constantly sloping angles. Rather than the typical radical exteriors of her early work, the Cincinnati museum is more subtle, more mature, and straightforward, yet completely original and interesting to view. The sophisticated façade forms a series of undulating translucent boxes in which passersby can peer into the life of the center. Once described as "wayward drawers on a piece of furniture,"[12] they enliven the corner on which the building sits, and project a three-dimensional feeling of a sculpture. An "urban carpet" which combines the public space, entrance and lobby are intended to draw in pedestrian movement. The outside ground curves slowly upward as it enters the building, leading visitors up to the mezzanine ramp suspended above the ground, which then continues to rise to the gallery entrance.

The exhibits themselves circulate through narrow slits in an unpredictable, zigzag pattern that gives the appearance of a 3-D jigsaw puzzle. The result is an animated, ebullient experience, at once futuristic yet accessible and highly

Zaha Hadid on Buildings

"**B**uildings," she says, "should keep you dry and feed the soul." She picks up a bottle plonked on her desk to explain how architecture has changed through time. "You cannot break this bottle. There is no other bottle. That's what they used to think, and that's changed. And if I contribute to that, great."

"Architecture is really about well-being. I think that people want to feel good in space . . . On the one hand it's shelter, but it's also about pleasure."

functional, offering the museum-goer a generous and remarkable spirit. "What is exciting about the Contemporary Arts Center," noted Hadid, "is the degree of unpredictability it involves. Unpredictability was actually part of the mandate we were given."[13]

Does the Cincinnati center usher in a new design phase for Hadid, or push her further into the mainstream? That remains to be seen. But what seems certain is that Hadid's place in the history of architecture is secure. As Pritzker Juror Rolf Fehlbaum noted, "Without *ever* building, Zaha Hadid would have radically expanded architecture's repertoire of spatial articulation. Now that the implementation in complex buildings is happening, the power of her innovation is fully revealed."[14]

Like so many of the Pritzker recipients who preceded her and, indeed, like the great architects of prior centuries, so much of what Hadid can envision is now able to be brought to fruition thanks to technical innovations. But more important, as Zaha Hadid fearlessly continues to pursue her strong personal vision, it will continue to "set new boundaries for the art of architecture."

As Harvard University's Jorge Silvetti stated, Hadid's "inimitable manipulation of walls, ground planes, and roofs, with those transparent, interwoven and fluid spaces, are vivid proof that architecture as a fine art has not run out of steam, and is hardly wanting of imagination."[15] It is in that spirit, that Zaha Hadid, the first female ever to receive the Pritzker Prize, fulfills the mission of this great honor and will continue to do it justice. ∎

"Every architect is — necessarily — a great poet. He must be a great original interpreter of his time, his day, his age."

— Frank Lloyd Wright

Architecture — A Mythical Fantastic

The talented architects featured in this book and, in fact, all Pritzker Prize winners, clearly live up to Wright's definition. They are all gifted artists. Their work is visual poetry, and they shape our lives — indeed our civilization — in new and exciting ways.

Though they may express their art in different styles, in varying shapes — or even in ways we never dreamed possible — they are united in their dedication to creating works of art that will inspire and uplift us in the places we live, work, play and worship. They endeavor, project by project, to move us by what we see, even though we often "look without seeing."

The architect Maya Ying Lin has described architecture "as a mythical fantastic. It has to be *experienced*. It can't be described. We can draw it up, and we can make models of it, but it can only be experienced as a complete whole." When looking back on the work of the Pritzker Prize winners, her message rings so true. Mere words cannot do the buildings justice. They indeed *must* be experienced to appreciate fully the artistic visions of the individual architects and to understand how they can affect our lives and our very souls.

Lin described architecture "as a mythical fantastic. It has to be *experienced*. It can't be described. We can draw it up, and we can make models of it, but it can only be experienced as a complete whole." — Maya Ying Lin

This booklet provides just a small sampling of the work, motivation and background of a handful of Pritzker Architecture Prize winners in an attempt to celebrate the contributions of *all* the winners to our culture, and to recognize the Hyatt Foundation for giving this unique art form its due. It's not *nearly* enough to do any of the architects justice, and it fails to showcase the wonderful work done by the Pritzker winners who have not been profiled. Nor does it adequately explain the nuances between the various schools of thought and differing styles of architecture, or how they have evolved over time. But it should serve to show the unifying traits that all the Pritzker honorees possess, which make them masters of their craft, and which affect our lives.

- They are all visionaries.
- They are risk-takers who create daring new images and relentlessly struggle to see their work realized.
- The are original thinkers who are unwilling to place limitations on their imaginations.
- Above all, heart and soul, they are artists.

In every form of artistic expression, modern practice builds upon its own past. Each architect learns from his or her predecessors and then charts his own course. The future of architecture, which will be reflected in the selection of Pritzker Prize Laureates yet to become, will certainly be controversial, experimental and varied. But they will all, to paraphrase historian Vincent Scully, continue to "build visible history." And as Frank Lloyd Wright foretold, they will surely be the most influential interpreters of their time . . . their day . . . their age. ■

Pritzker Architecture Prize Winners: 1979-2004

1979 **Philip Johnson,** United States
presented at Dumbarton Oaks, Washington DC

1980 **Luis Barragán,** Mexico
presented at Dumbarton Oaks, Washington DC

1981 **James Stirling,** Great Britain
presented at the National Building Museum, Washington DC

1982 **Kevin Roche,** United States
presented at The Art Institute, Chicago, Illinois

1983 **Ieoh Ming Pei,** United States
presented at the National Gallery of Art, Washington DC

1984 **Richard Meier,** United States
presented at the National Gallery of Art, Washington DC

1985 **Hans Hollein,** Austria
presented at the Huntington Library, Art Collections and
Botanical Gardens, San Marino, California

1986 **Gottfried Böhm,** Germany
presented at Goldsmiths' Hall, London, England

1987 **Kenzo Tange,** Japan
presented at the Kimball Art Museum, Fort Worth, Texas

1988 **Gordon Nunshaft,** United States
Oscar Niemeyer, Brazil
presented at The Art Institute, Chicago, Illinois

1989 **Frank Gehry,** United States
presented at Todaiji Buddhist Temple, Nara, Japan

1990 **Aldo Rossi,** Italy
presented at Palazzo Grassi, Venice, Italy

1991 **Robert Venturi,** United States
presented at Palacio de Iturbidi, Mexico City, Mexico

1992 **Álvaro Siza,** Portugal
presented at the Harold Washington Library Center, Chicago, Illinois

1993 **Fumihiko Maki,** Japan
presented at Prague Castle, Czech Republic

1994 **Christian de Portzamparc,** France
presented at The Commons, Columbus, Indiana

1995 **Tadao Ando,** Japan
presented at the Grand Trianon and Chateau of Versailles, France

1996 **Rafael Moneo,** Spain
presented at the construction site of The Getty Center,
Los Angeles, California

1997 **Sverre Fehn,** Norway
presented at the construction site of The Guggenheim Museum,
Bilbao, Spain

1998 **Renzo Piano,** Italy
presented at The White House, Washington, DC

1999	**Sir Norman Foster,** Great Britain presented at the Altus Museum, Berlin, Germany
2000	**Rem Koolhaas,** The Netherlands presented at the Jerusalem Archeological Park, Israel
2001	**Jacques Herzog,** Switzerland **Pierre de Meuron,** Switzerland presented at Thomas Jefferson's Monticello, Virginia
2002	**Glenn Murcutt,** Australia presented at Michelangelo's Campidoglio, Rome, Italy
2003	**Jørn Utzon,** Denmark presented at The Royal Academy of Fine Arts of San Fernando, Madrid, Spain
2004	**Zaha Hadid,** Great Britain presented at St. Petersburg, Russia

Reprinted from www.pritzkerprize.com with permission, The Hyatt Foundation.

Notes and Photo Credits

INTRODUCTION

1 Reprinted from www.pritzkerprize.com with permission, The Hyatt Foundation
2 "Jerusalem Archaeological Park Provides 2000-Year-Old Site for Pritzker Prize," at www.pritzkerprize.com

CHAPTER 1

1 "Philip Johnson's Acceptance Speech," at www.pritzkerprize.com
2 "Philip Johnson, Dean of American Architects," February 28, 1992, at www.achievements.org
3 "Philip Johnson's Acceptance Speech," *Op. Cit.*
4 "Philip Johnson, Dean of American Architects," *Op. Cit.*
5 "Master Builders," 1985, John Wiley
6 "Designs Moving Forward for 'urban glass house'"—*Real Estate Weekly*, March 31, 2004

CHAPTER 2

1 Quoted in Anada Alanis, Clasico del Silencio, Escala (publisher), 1989
2 "The Houses of Luis Barragán," *Mexico Connect*, 1989
3 "The Houses of Luis Barragán," *Mexico Connect*, 1989
4 "Barragán," Rizzoli, 1992
5 *Ibid*
6 Jackie Craven, *Luis* Barragán *House*, 2004, www.architecture.about.com

[7] Carlos Agestra, "Casa Luis Barragán: Poetry of Color," *Architecture Week*, November, 2000 (translated by Anna Bonta from May, 2000 issue of *Architectural Digital*)

[8] Karen K. Alexander, AIA, "Defining Yourself," at *ISdesigNET Magazine*, July/August, 2003

[9] The Houses of Luis Barragán," *Mexico Connect*, 1989

[10] *Ibid*

[11] "Barragán," Rizzoli, 1992

[12] Luis Barragán, in Muriel Emanuel (Ed.), *Contemporary Architects,* St.Martin's Press, 1988

CHAPTER 3

[1] Laureate profiles, at www.pritzkerprize.com

[2] *Ibid*

[3] *Ibid*

[4] Richard Meier, *Richard Meier, Architect*, Oxford University Press, 1976

[5] Richard Meier, *Op. Cit.*

[6] Laureate profiles, at www.pritzkerprize.com

[7] Laureate profiles, at www.pritzkerprize.com

[8] Betsy Malloy, Getty Museum Architecture, Visitor Guide to the Getty Museum

[9] Peter Gaito, Jr, "Apartments outside the Box," *Architecture Week*, October 16, 2002

CHAPTER 4

[1] "Gallery of Architectural Quotations," *Ergoarchitecture*

[2] Karen Templer, Frank Gehry, for Salon.com, July 18, 2004

[3] *Ibid*

[4] "Frank Gehry's Acceptance Speech," at www.pritzkerprize.com

[5] Ada Louise Huxtabel, "On Awarding the Prize," at www.pritzkerprize.com

[6] Karen Templer, Frank Gehry, for Salon.com, July 18, 2004

[7] "Frank Gehry's Acceptance Speech," at www.pritzkerprize.com

[8] "Guggenheim Museum Bilbao," *CultureVenture*, May 30, 2001

[9] "Gallery of Architectural Quotations," Ergo Architecture

[10] "Frank O. Gehry Walt Disney Concert Hall," *ArcSpace*, October 20, 2003

[11] "Frank O. Gehry Walt Disney Concert Hall," *ArcSpace*, October 20, 2003

[12] Jennifer Barrett, "Master Builder," MSNBC/Newsweek Society, April 16, 2004

[13] Karen Templer, Frank Gehry, for Salon.com, July 18, 2004

[14] *Ibid*

[15] "Gehry's Cleveland Landmark," Case Western Reserve University, www.cwru.edu

CHAPTER 5

1 Vittorio Gregotti, "Thoughts on the Works of Álvaro Siza," at www.pritzkerprize.com
2 "About Álvaro Siza, 1992, at www.pritzkerprize.com
3 "Robert Venturi," at www.pritzkerprize.com
4 "Architect Robert Venturi," Great Buildings Online,
5 "Citation from the Pritzker jury," at www.pritzkerprize.com
6 "Citation from the Pritzker Jury," at www.pritzkerprize.com
7 "Álvaro Siza: Santa Maria Church," *ArcSpace.com*
8 "Fumihiko Maki," www.pritzkerprize.com
9 *Casabella Magazine*, July, 1986
10 Cited at *Editorial Blau*, www.cidadevirtual.pt, 1995

CHAPTER 6

1 "Tadao Ando name 1995 Laureate," at www.pritzkerprize.com
2 Tadao Ando with Werner Blaser, *Sketches*, Springer Verlag, 1989
3 "Tadao Ando named 1995 Laureate," at www.pritzkerprize.com
4 "Tadao Ando: A Master of Mystical Places,"Carolyn Armenta Davis, *ISDesignet*
5 Simon Glynn, 2001, at www.galinsky.com
6 "Art of Ando in St. Louis," *Architecture Week*, October, 2001
7 "Ando's New Modern," *Architecture Week*, January 2003
8 *Ibid*
9 *Ibid*
10 "Citation from the Jury," at www.pritzkerprize.com
11 "Tadao Ando interview," *designboom*, October 2001
12 Carolyn Armenta Davis, "Tadao Ando" A Master of Mystical Places," ISdesig.NET Magazine, September, 1995

CHAPTER 7

1 "Master Builder," *Online NewsHour*, June, 1998
2 "About Renzo Piano," www.pritzkerprize.com
3 Leonard R. Bachman, "Systematic Centre Pompidou," *Architecture Week*, December, 2003
4 "Citation from the Jury," www.pritzkerprize.com
5 *Ibid*
6 Piano, Renzo, *InfoPlease*
7 "Renzo Piano, The Architect's Studio," *ArcSpace*
8 "About Renzo Piano," www.pritzkerprize.com

9   *Ibid*

10 *Ibid*

CHAPTER 8

1   "About Sir Norman Foster," Pritzker Prize media kit, www.pritzkerprize.com

2   "Norman Foster: Foster and Partners," *designboom*, September 2001

3   "Norman Foster: Foster and Partners," *designboom*, September 2001

4   "Citation from the Pritzker Prize Jury," www.pritzkerprize.com

5   *Ibid*

6   "About Sir Norman Foster," Pritzker Prize media kit, www.pritzkerprize.com

7   *Ibid*

8   *Ibid*

9   *Ibid*

10 "About Sir Norman Foster," Pritzker Prize media kit, www.pritzkerprize.com

11 "Features, Ideas, Architecture, Interview: Sir Norman Foster," *Christian Science Monitor*, April 15, 1999

12 About Sir Norman Foster," Pritzker Prize media kit, www.pritzkerprize.com

13 Michael J. Crosbie, "Norman Foster: Analog and Digital Ecology," *Architecture Week*, September 2000

14 "Features, Ideas, Architecture, Interview: Sir Norman Foster," *Christian Science Monitor*, April 15, 1999

15 "About Sir Norman Foster," Pritzker Prize media kit, www.pritzkerprize.com

16 "Norman Foster: Foster and Partners," *designboom*, September 2001

17 "Swiss Re Headquarters," www.fosterandpartners.com

18 "Norman Foster: Foster and Partners," *designboom*, September 2001

19 "Jury Citation," www.pritzkerprize.com

CHAPTER 9

1   "Rem Koolhaas," Pritzker Architecture Prize Laureate, at www.pritzkerprize.com

2   Lynn Becker, "About Rem Koolhaas," *the Chicago Reader*, September 26, 2003

3   "Rem Koolhaas of the Netherlands," at www.pritzkerprize.com

4   Lynn Becker, "About Rem Koolhaas," *the Chicago Reader*, September 26, 2003

5   *Ibid*

6   "Rem Koolhaas, biography," Illinois Institute of Technology, at www.iit.edu

7   Phyllis Lambert, founding director, Canadian Centre of Architecture, Montreal, cited in "About Rem Koolhaas, *Ibid*.

8   "Citation from the Pritzker Prize Jury," at www.pritzkerprize.com

9   Marcus Fairs, "Rem Koolhaas," *Icon Magazine*, June, 2004

[10] "About Rem Koolhaas," *Op. Cit.*

[11] Rem Koohlaas, "McCormick Tribune Campus Center," *arcspace.com*

[12] *Ibid*

[13] *Ibid*

[14] Marcus Fairs, "Rem Koolhaas," *Icon Magazine,* June, 2004

[15] Images, *archphoto*

[16] Paul Goldberger, "High-tech Bibliophilia," *The New Yorker*, May 24, 2004

[17] Marcus Fairs, "Rem Koolhaas," *Icon Magazine,* June, 2004

[18] "The New Seattle Library: A monument to literacy," *The Week*, June 4, 2004

[19] Ingrid Sischy, "Rem Koolhaas," *Interview*, October, 2000

[20] Paul Goldberger, "High-tech Bibliophilia," *The New Yorker*, May 24, 2004

[21] Marcus Fairs, "Rem Koolhaas," *Icon Magazine,* June, 2004

CHAPTER 10

[1] Simon Hattenstone, "Master Builder," *The Guardian*, February 3, 2003

[2] Ada Louise Huxtable, Pritzker Jury, 2004

[3] "Deconstructing Hadid," by Christopher Hawthorne, *Slate*, March 2004

[4] Simon Hattenstone, "Master Builder," *The Guardian,* February 3, 2003

[5] Christopher Hawthorne, "Deconstructing Hadid," *Slate*, March, 2003

[6] *Ibid*

[7] "Zaha Hadid," ArBitat

[8] Christian Horn, "Hadid's Bergisel Ski Jump," *Architecture Week*, May, 2003

[9] Katherine Logan, "British AIA Awards 2002," *Architecture Week*, April, 2002

[10] *Ibid*

[11] Christopher Hawthorne, "Deconstructing Hadid," *Slate*, March, 2003

[12] *Ibid*

[13] Zaha Hadid, "Contemporary Arts Center," at www.arcspace.com

[14] "Citation from the Jury," at www.pritzkerprize.com

[15] *Ibid*

Photo Credits

CHAPTER 1: Johnson
The Glass House: Richard Bryant/arcaid.co.uk
Penzoil Place: Mary Ann Sullivan, Bluffton University
AT&T Headquarters: Mary Ann Sullivan, Bluffton University
Crystal Cathedral: John Edward Linden/arcaid.co.uk

CHAPTER 2: Barragán
Casa de Luis Barragán: Pedro Bonta/ArchitectureWeek.com
Interior of Casa de Luis Barragán (Back of Main Room):
    Pedro Bonta/ArchitectureWeek.com
Interior of Casa de Luis Barragán: Pedro Bonta/ArchitectureWeek.com

CHAPTER 3: Meier
The High Museum of Art — Atlanta, Georgia: Mary Ann Sullivan, Bluffton University
The Getty Center: Anthony Abbate, AIA
Perry Street Towers: Peter Gaito, Jr./ArchitectureWeek.com

CHAPTER 4: Gehry
Frank Gehry's Residence: Anthony Abbate, AIA
Chiat/Day Office: Anthony Abbate, AIA
The Guggenheim Museum — Bilbao, Spain: Anthony Abbate, AIA
Walt Disney Concert Hall: John Edward Linden/arcaid.co.uk

CHAPTER 5: Siza
Meteorology Center: arcspace.com

CHAPTER 6: Ando
Church of Light: arcspace.com
Modern Art Museum of Fort Worth: Mary Ann Sullivan, Bluffton University

CHAPTER 7: Piano
Georges Pompidou Center: Anthony Abbate, AIA
The Menil Collection: Mary Ann Sullivan, Bluffton University
Nasher Center: John Edward Linden/arcaid.co.uk

CHAPTER 8: Foster
Hong Kong Airport: Richard Bryant/arcaid.co.uk
New Paliament Reichstag — Germany: Anthony Abbate, AIA
Swiss Re Headquarters: Anthony Abbate, AIA

CHAPTER 9: Koolhaas
McCormick Tribune Campus Center: floto+warner-arcaid/architekturphoto
Lille Grand Palais: Ralph Richter/architekturphoto
Seattle Central Library: arcspace.com

CHAPTER 10: Hadid
Bergisel Ski Jump Tower: Architekturphoto/arcaid.co.uk

Recommended
Reading

Recommended Reading

Building Codes Illustrated
A Guide to Understanding the International Building Codes
By Ching and Winkel

Building Codes Illustrated combines highly illustrative explanations with expert guidance to provide an accessible, timesaving companion guide to the new International Building Code® (IBC). Understanding the criteria for code development and the reasons for code provisions is essential to unlocking this unified code. Organized to correspond with related subject matter in the IBC, Building Codes Illustrated enables architects, engineers, and other design professionals to quickly find clarifying information on the nonstructural provisions of the IBC and gain a clear and complete understanding of those sections at a glance through enlightening computer-rendered illustrations and succinct, thorough interpretations.

$45.00 Item# BC95x1037970

Architectural Graphic Standards, 10th Edition
By Charles G. Ramsey

For over 70 years, Architectural Graphic Standards has been the bedrock design reference for generations of architects, builders and engineers. Now comes the most complete design tool yet — the completely updated and expanded Tenth Edition. You'll find a wealth of information, completed with 10,000 drawings. Each of the 1,092 pages in the Tenth Edition is a fully self-contained data sheet, detailing standard materials, installation and design configurations, and recommended performance specifications for the pertinent building system or component.

$250.00 Item# BC95x32554

www.ArchitectureBookDeals.com

Interior Graphic Standards
By McGowan and Kruse

The interior construction of a building includes everything inside of the structural shell — from interior partitions and floor systems to wall covering and carpeting. With over 3,000 illustrations, this book is the most complete and authoritative professional reference on interior construction available, and is the definitive interior design reference that the industry has been waiting for.

$199.00 Item# BC95x1161670

Architect's Professional Practice Manual
By James R. Franklin

This book is a no-nonsense compendium of well-tested methods, valuable tips, contracts, forms, checklists, and other tools in a graphics-oriented and at-a-glance format. Beginning with how to position yourself in the marketplace, it takes you through the entire process of marketing, pricing, negotiating, designing, and carrying out projects, showing you how to build repeat client business while maintaining your joy and profitability through exemplary practices.

$59.95 Item# BC95x44725

Architectural Formulas Pocket Reference
By Robert Brown Butler

This extremely portable reference provides instant access to more than 1,100 architectural equations, and offers all you need to know to design buildings that work successfully. Whether your architectural concerns are structural, climate control, plumbing, electrical, illumination, acoustics, or general design, this distillation of many larger volumes of architectural engineering science will lay the foundation for the design of any building — from shed to skyscraper anywhere in the world — that will satisfy designer and client alike.

$39.95 Item# BC95x91526

■ ■ ■

www.ArchitectureBookDeals.com

Architect's Essentials of Starting a Design Firm
By Perkins and Piven

This essential volume offers a step-by-step guide to understanding and evaluating the goals, risks and the rewards of starting a firm. It covers the basics of firm organization, personnel requirements, legal considerations, fee setting, marketing issues, and the essentials of strategic and business plans. In addition, it also addresses how to get started — including how to create your first business plan, evaluate initial needs and costs, create a budget, and produce a list of action items. This volume is practical, applied, concise, portable, affordable, and user-friendly.

$35.00 Item# BC95x956656

Interior Design Visual Presentation
A Guide to Graphics, Models & Presentation Techniques, 2nd Edition
By Maureen Mitton

The new, updated edition is fully revised to include the latest material on CAD, digital portfolios, resume preparation, and Web page design. It remains the only comprehensive guide to address the visual design and presentation needs of the interior designer, with coverage of design graphics, models, and presentation techniques in one complete volume. Approaches to the planning, layout, and design of interior spaces are presented through highly visual, step-by-step instructions, supplemented with more than forty pages of full-color illustrations, exercises at the end of each chapter, and dozens of new projects. With the serious designer in mind, it includes a diverse range of sample work — from student designers as well as well-known design firms such as Ellerbee and Beckett Architects and MS Architects.

$45.00 Item# BC95x1174534

Architect's Portable Handbook
By John P. Guthrie

This ultimate reference guide details information from construction costs and building laws to lighting and drainage. Thousands of checklists, codes, formulas, and techniques are at your fingertips so you can get the most accurate information available. An excellent tool for design professionals of any kind!

$59.95 Item# BC95x1036693

Architects on Architects

By Goldberger and Gray

Here's a profound, stirring study of how the world's greatest architects influenced the work of others and why—told in the architects' own dramatic and awe-filled words. The contributors discuss the career-inspiring achievements of their mentors, designers of some of the most famous structures on earth. They delve into their own design philosophy, and how the genius of others affected their careers, their goals, as well as their lives. Each original essay is beautifully illustrated with photographs of both the architect's work and that of his mentor, providing a visually stunning forum for comparison and learning.

$39.95 Item# BC95x45074

Introduction to Landscape Design

By John Motloch

Outstanding explorations of design concepts, principles, and processes, this Second Edition offers even broader coverage of the environmental, human, technological, and aesthetic issues associated with landscape design than the First Edition. Beginning with the way we perceive, manage, and design the landscape, it moves on to explore the forces that influence land design. The book is an excellent guide for anyone who wants to develop a better understanding of landscape design.

$70.00 Item# BC95x32609

■ ■ ■

www.ArchitectureBookDeals.com

About the Authors

Jaye Abbate is a publishing and marketing professional. She has extensive experience producing and marketing a wide range of products including books, magazines, newsletters and videos, and has written articles, book reviews and booklets on numerous topics. She is a graduate of Northwestern University, and lives in Fort Lauderdale, Florida.

Michael C. Thomsett is author of over 60 books throughout his career to date. His best-selling *Getting Started in Options* (John Wiley & Sons) has sold over 180,000 copies. Thomsett has also written books with Dearborn, Amacom, and many other publishers; and has worked on many projects with Marketplace Books, Inc. He lives in Port Townsend, Washington.